The Mighty and the Mysterious will fill you with wonder, refresh your heart, and redirect your life. With scholarship, humor, meaning, insight, and some sass, Heidi Goehmann helps Paul's powerful Letter to the Colossians live in you and through you. Tackling tough issues, Heidi takes you on a heartfelt journey to grow as one who is "in Christ" and in community with His precious people. This user-friendly Bible study has stimulating questions and faith-building features that will bless, inspire, and renew your walk with Jesus.

—Rev. Michael Newman, author of *Hope When Your Heart Breaks: Navigating Grief and Loss* (CPH, 2017), president, Texas District LCMS

In *The Mighty and the Mysterious*, Heidi leads us in such a way that we almost forget she's there. We are drawn by the Holy Spirit to walk so deeply through this study: learning, digging, and discovering how mighty and how mysterious God truly is. Heidi's gift to teach puts us in a confident position to learn and understand the context and vocabulary of Colossians as well as that great second language: "Christianese." Whether you are a seasoned biblical scholar, someone like myself (no college degree), or someone in between, Heidi's new study will prepare and challenge you.

—Mia Koehne, singer and recording artist, cofounder of Aspire Women's Events

Heidi Goe_ love for the Church, in particular, is bigger than anyone else's I have ever seen. In her new study, *The Mighty and the Mysterious*, Heidi combines her passion for the Church with her love for God's Word. Readers discover that the Letter to the Colossians wasn't just for the Early Church. It's also for us today. In this flexible six-week study, you will see God's plan for His Church and for you, and you will learn what life together in Christ looks like.

—Matthew Wingert, theology teacher, Orange Lutheran High School

Heidi's study of Colossians is a walk through the nitty-gritty reality of life, the suffering and discomfort we face every day, and the simultaneous incredible wonder that our God and Savior walks beside us and before us through it all. This study connects to so many levels of the daily Christian life. Along the way, Heidi encourages you to keep asking questions, keep reading Scripture, and keep living in the mighty and mysterious love that God has for His children. Take your time as you walk through this journey.

—Christel Neuendorf, deaconess and missionary, LCMS Office of International Mission

THE Mighty & THE Mysterious

A STUDY OF COLOSSIANS
by HEIDI GOEHMANN

Concordia
Publishing House

Founded in 1869 as the publishing arm of The Lutheran Church—Missouri Synod, Concordia Publishing House gives all glory to God for the blessing of 150 years of opportunities to provide resources that are faithful to the Holy Scriptures and the Lutheran Confessions.

Published by Concordia Publishing House
3558 S. Jefferson Avenue, St. Louis, MO 63118-3968
1-800-325-3040 ● cph.org

Text copyright © 2019 by Heidi Goehmann
Artwork by Brooke Gettman © 2019 Concordia Publishing House

Manufactured in the United States of America

1 2 3 4 5 6 7 8 9 10   28 27 26 25 24 23 22 21 20 19

To the Church on earth:
You are a wild, messy, worthwhile, beautiful, complicated,
encouraging, frustrating, mighty, mysterious gift.

I love you.
I can't deal with you.
I was made for you.
You bring me heartache.
You give me joy.
You are His and that is enough.

Contents

Introduction

This last year, our family took a trip to Winnipeg in Manitoba, Canada.

We haphazardly chose this destination because it was within a day's drive of our house, held the opportunity to see some hockey, and had economical hotel options in the city center. As a bonus, it was international and we all had our passports. When the time came for our trip, we packed the van to the brim with a bin of ice skates and a duffel bag bulging with extra mittens, hats, scarves, and long underwear; grabbed our bag of audiobooks from the library; and put pedal to the metal to jet out of town.

It was a long drive, but as soon as we crossed the border, I kid you not the air became sweeter—not because Canadians have cleaner air, but because my children stopped bickering and busied themselves instead with gawking out the windows to see what looked different in Manitoba compared with our native Nebraskaland. Once we arrived in Winnipeg itself, our children started to holler out the fun and festive landmarks:

"Ooooo! There's a giant Canadian flag."

"Ohhh! That's the capital building!"

"They have Korean food here!"

"Look, there's the art museum!"

"It's so metropolitan!"

But then we got out of our car . . . and were greeted by The Slush.

I can't even begin to describe the level of slush in this city. We trudged and we trekked through miles of it as we explored and adventured. We had forgotten our winter boots, and every time you heard someone yell, "Oh man!" you knew it meant he or she had been trying to sidestep a puddle and the puddle had won.

On that first day of adventuring, finding ourselves at the place between shivering uncontrollably and the beginning stages of frostnip, we rounded a corner to see a park full of people chatting, laughing, and skating as sunshine streamed on them from the March sky. We all stood speechless for a moment, taking it in.

In the city of Winnipeg, where the Red and Assiniboine Rivers meet, you can skate the Red River Mutual Trail, one of the longest naturally occurring frozen skating paths in the world. Part of this trail is surrounded by city buildings, overpasses, and pedestrian bridges. Still more is surrounded by overhanging trees, wide open fields of snow, and the biggest slice of sky you can imagine. There is also a sense of stunning community along the trail. The city comes alive with hockey rinks, warming huts, and benches all along the path. There are people skating with dogs, toddlers in strollers, young couples on first dates, and families all around, any time of day.

Our skates strapped on, we joined in the community, discovering the frozen wonderland. After an hour, I was stiff, a little tired, but a lot amazed. I looked around me—

God created all of this?

He created the river that flowed four inches below my feet. He created the bright sunshine that warmed my face. He created snow that blinded my eyes with its whiteness. He created not just water, but He cleverly created ice as well. He created, and then He created some more.

He created the laughter of my daughter as she zipped ahead of me and urged me to go faster. He created the arms of the dad supporting plump little feet learning to skate. He created friendship and the sweat of middle school boys running off the incessant energy that comes with growing. He created the fire that warms and the community that grows around it.

There is a God who creates—making life, heartbeats, a world to discover, and all the pieces in it. And then He knits and knits and knits. Each day He is making afghans of connection and community. They warm us and point us right back to the beginning—to our Father, to His Son, and to His Spirit, who are weaving plans and purposes into this whole big blanket we call life.

As I stood on the Red River Mutual Trail, the big, bold, beautiful realization of what God has created and what He continues to create amazed me. But the realization that He is intimately connected to His creation and that He intricately connects His creation left me reverberating with shock. And it led me to the Book of Colossians.

Colossians gives us a vantage point to see this deep connection between our Savior and His people, between our Savior and everything He has created across time and places and spaces.

Jesus was there in the beginning of all this creating, and He's still working now. He is the great connector. He connects every piece, one to another. In the day-to-day of life, many times we see the slush rather than the clear, smooth, beautiful surface of the Red River Mutual Trail. The slush makes life confusing. One minute we're experiencing car games and a fun time, the next our feet are ankle deep in a dark blob of cold, wet questions without answers. We try to sidestep these questions, but there's a crowd of pedestrians and a street full of traffic and sometimes our only option is to walk through the slush and murkiness. The slush can make it difficult to see Jesus working in our lives, the connections He is making all around us and the redemption He is bringing to our moments and our relationships.

Colossians reminds us that God is mighty, even in the midst of our slush.

He is also mysterious. He doesn't always clean up the slush, the questions. But He does walk us through it. Those questions, if we let them, will connect us deeper to Him and to one another. That connection is joy and peace in our lives, even when we can't see the path He is making.

He is marvelous, majestic, merciful, and always meaningful.

Jesus Christ is Creator and Connector. He is the mighty and the mysterious.

How to Use This Study

We often make God too small or too large. Colossians teaches us that God is big and mighty but also that, in Christ and through the Spirit, God is accessible to us. Colossians teaches us that God knits us together with the whole Body of Christ and that, through His Word, He reveals to us what we need to know to be in true relationship with Him and with one another. All of this is mighty, and it is mysterious.

Because we all are in different seasons and places in our walk with this mighty and mysterious God, this Bible study is designed to meet you where you are, with lots of options for accountability with flexibility:

Option 1—Each week, there are five days of study included in this workbook. Maybe you are giddy with excitement to dig in to all of this, or maybe it is intimidating as you page through. In Christ, it's all about grace—so you decide how you'd like to proceed through this workbook. There is no one right way. I want to encourage you to be in the Word on a daily basis, but that can look different depending on your stage or season of life. Each "day" in this workbook should take about thirty minutes to complete. Some people like to sit down and do more than one day at a time. Others like to schedule a set time each day as study time. Still others spend time focusing on two questions in a day's study, and then they set it aside and come back to the rest of the day's study on the following day. You can commit to completing one of the study days each week or two, three, four, or all five of the days. Remember, this is grace-based. Some weeks in life are busier than others. So do what you can. God will speak through His Word, no matter how much of this workbook you are able to read and complete.

Option 2—Watch the video segment connected with each week of study, whether as an individual or with a study group. Video downloads can be found at cph.org/mightymysterious. You can use the workbook without the videos and not feel like you're missing huge chunks. But the videos offer another opportunity for you to learn and for a group to learn and discuss Colossians together. The videos make it easier for you to lead a study group, if you want to study with others. If all you can commit to in this season of life is watching the videos with a group or on your own, and skipping over the rest of the workbook, the Word is still at work! You will not feel behind in the study if you do not watch the videos, but you will miss some really great content, if I do say so myself!

Option 3—This workbook includes fun facts, bonus articles, white space for journaling and prayer requests, Bible verses to contemplate and memorize, and artwork to meditate on. Be creative with it. Share a picture or post on social media of what you're learning or enjoying in this study. Consider what parts of this study would be a message of hope that you could share in someone else's day. Frame the art on your fridge or wall. Write out Bible verses you like and put them in places you'll see them often to remind you of your redemption in Christ. The sky is the limit!

My one recommendation is, if at all possible, to *gather* with others for this study—whether in person, over the phone, online, via video chat, or via text messages. The Book of Colossians will make you hungry for real, genuine community. There are times when it is very valuable and helpful to study God's Word alone with our Savior by the Holy Spirit. But as we will learn in our study, God intended us to do life *together* in Christ. Our lives can feel very isolating at times. I don't want you to find yourself massively lonely as you study Colossians, where you'll discover God's wondrous work of connecting us with one another in the Body of Christ. Having a friend or a group to share and discuss with as we study God's Word reminds us that we are part of the Church, and that the Church on earth has a purpose: we are meant to suffer together and to rejoice together and to show Jesus to one another. Let's start today.

Suggestions for Facilitating This Study in a Group

You are surrounded by a great cloud of witnesses doing this study alongside you! Think about all of the groups around the country (and even the world) holding this same book, walking through God's Word together. Isn't that cool?! That doesn't mean, though, that every study group will look the same.

Here are some ideas as you consider how to facilitate your group. These come from other facilitators who found that these strategies helped their group dig into God's Word and often led to fruitful, open conversation together:

- Cultivate an environment of grace. Let participants know there are rarely right or wrong answers in this study. Instead, help them understand that the goal of this study is questions and open discussion around the Word. We all are trying to figure out life and faith. Being together in God's Word is the best place to wrestle with questions we all have about faith, people, heartache, and life-size and everyday challenges. Invite kind and loving disagreement between study members. Not everyone will agree with the author or with one another at all times. Help people frame their thoughts within an environment of safety and grace, recognizing that the multiple perspectives people bring to a small group are powerful gifts. Allow the group to have mild tangents in discussion and reflection. Members of the group need time to get to know one another in order to be able to grow together and start to do life together.

- Ask the question, "What did you find interesting in this week's study?" to start the discussion when your group gathers. It's always fun to see what stuck out to other people during their alone study time.

- As you do your own alone study time for the days in the workbook, put an asterisk or other mark next to the study segments or questions you find most interesting. Bring these up the next time your group gathers, to help spark discussion. If you found it interesting, chances are someone else will too!

- When I facilitate groups with video studies, I structure our time like this: take prayer requests, have prayer time, discuss the previous week's study work, then watch the video and discuss the video. But *any* order works. Whatever works for your group is the right way for your group. It's also okay to go at a slower pace, doing one week of study over a month's time, or whatever sounds best to your group.

- During your group discussion, spend time studying at least two or three of the Bible verses from the previous week's study days. Some participants may not be able to spend much time in the Word outside of your group meeting time. So give them the chance to meditate on God's Word by doing so as a group during some of your meeting time. Even if someone has already focused on those verses during the week, it never hurts to return to the same Scripture verses multiple times. God opens our eyes to new insights every time.

- There will likely be questions that you or others leave blank during the course of the study. Some questions speak to certain people more than others. Perhaps consider challenging one another to answer the questions that are most *uncomfortable* first. But know that it is also very normal and okay to skip questions sometimes as well.

- Pay attention to the extras each week and the boxes in the margin, particularly if you are looking for an "answer" or for more information on the text or a certain idea.

- Appoint a "scribe" who takes really great notes during the video. This way if someone misses a point or a fill-in, they won't need to feel stressed out during the video. And the scribe's video notes can be a helpful resource during your group's discussion of the video.

- Ask a youngin' in your group to help with the technology if you hit a roadblock. We have many different gifts in the church. You might be shocked at how crazy knowledgeable young people are about technology things. And there's no reason to repeatedly want to throw your computer out of the window. ☺

Repeat this to yourself, "There is no one *right way* to do Bible study." The only *right way* is to gather around the inerrant Word of God and to keep searching for His truth and love with the help of His Spirit and with Jesus, our Savior, as our foundation.

Happy studying, friends!

Asia Minor

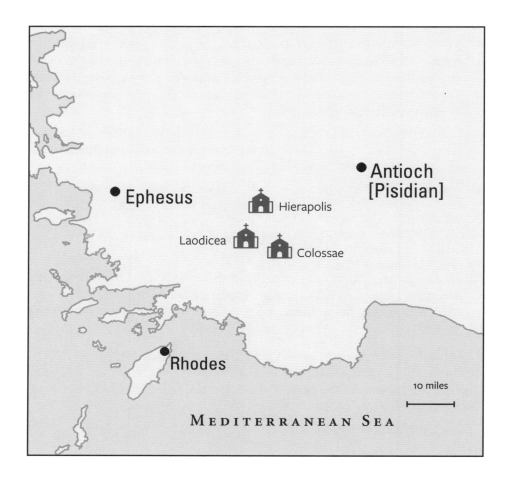

In Paul's Letter to the Colossians, he also mentions the cities of Laodicea and Hierapolis. There was a trio of churches between Colossae, Laodicea, and Hierapolis, within fifteen miles of one another. Though Paul had never visited any of those churches before he wrote his Letter to the Colossians, these three churches were all fruits of the church Paul planted in Ephesus.

Useful Terms

asceticism—the harsh discipline of the body for religious reasons, such as the avoidance of foods, beating the body, or other ways to deny the flesh in order to prove rejection of the things of the world and prioritization of the things of God. Asceticism is often also coupled with false humility.

Body of Christ—a uniquely descriptive and biblical phrase for the Church. This phrase refers to the people of God, knit together by His Spirit, with Jesus Christ as the head of the Body. Through this image, God gives us a picture of how the Church grows—intimately connected to the head, Jesus—and how it functions as a united Body made up of a diverse group of members. Jesus is the intimate connection and connector of all of us who are in the Church.

Christology—the study of the person, characteristics, work, and nature of Jesus Christ. Jesus is both fully God and fully a man, who walked on the earth and suffered and died for our sake.

community—a group of people living life together, whether because of close proximity, mutual interests, or other common bonds. In this book, I reserve the word *community* for the goal and process of genuine life together, rather than a vague idea of locality or grouping. Genuine community is living life together in authenticity—where accountability and individual gifts are valued, but also where mistakes, forgiveness, and grace are understood as necessary. In genuine life together, growth is valued over perfection. This meaning of *community* is the goal, however imperfect our experience of it might be.

cosmology—the study of the beginning, or the origin, of the universe and all that is in it—including plants, continents, constellations, oceans, and people.

Epistle—a fancy word for "letter"; a handwritten note used to communicate information and thoughts.

eschatology—the study of the end times; particularly, the study of how God will resolve the brokenness of the world and will usher in the new creation when Jesus returns.

evolution—the belief that all that exists developed and diversified over time through a very slow process of simpler microorganisms and cells becoming more complex beings.

flesh—the whole physical being of a person; it refers specifically to the meaty parts of human beings, what exists between skin and bones.

gnostic(s)—those who follow the teachings of Gnosticism, such as the belief that Jesus was a single representation of the divine and that humans need special knowledge to release the divine within themselves as well. Gnosticism teaches that all material, physical things are evil, while spiritual things are good.

heresy—a teaching, belief, theory, or opinion that is contrary to what Scripture teaches. A broad definition of *heresy* can be any teachings, beliefs, theories, or opinions that are against an established custom or religious belief. But for the purposes of our study, we will use the narrower definition of *heresy* as anything that is contrary to the teachings in the Bible.

preeminence—that which is supreme, having inarguable leadership, authority, and superiority; that which completely surpasses all other things. Jesus' preeminence means that He is Lord and Master of the universe and of our hearts and lives.

spirit—the parts of human beings that are not our flesh—what is not physical, such as our personality, our soul, our emotions, and our character.

the Colossian heresy—a collection of false teachings among the Christians in Colossae. Some of these teachings included the need to worship a pantheon of spirits in addition to worshiping Jesus; restrictions or requirements concerning rituals, feast days, and special celebrations; and the need to obtain higher, special knowledge about God beyond the Gospel of Jesus in order to become closer to God.

vocation—a calling, professionally, personally, or in family life. People have many vocations: daughter, brother, husband, mother, teacher, neighbor, friend, business manager, barista, and so forth. These vocations are not our identity but rather areas of life in which we serve and are able to give glory to God. Vocations can change with seasons of life. Our identity never changes: we are children of God, redeemed by Christ Jesus.

worldview—a lens by which we see the world around us, including our experiences, our relationships, and our communities. Our worldview also determines how we understand all the good, the bad, and the ugly of the world.

Week 1

ALL THAT IS MIGHTY

Viewer Guide

VERSES TO BOOKMARK
Colossians 4:7–17

VIDEO 1: WHAT'S UP WITH WORLDVIEW?—
AN OVERVIEW OF COLOSSIANS
COLOSSIANS 1:1–14

THE VALUE OF WORLDVIEW

WORLDVIEW
A lens by which we see
the world around us,
including our experiences,
our relationships, and our
communities. Our world-
view also determines how
we understand all the good,
the bad, and the ugly of the
world.

If our worldview isn't grounded in Scripture, we end up making things
_____ that aren't _____.

POSSIBLE PLANKS IN THE RAFT OF OUR WORLDVIEW*

- Plank—Who am I and where did I come from?
- Plank—Do I have a purpose?
- Plank—What does a healthy family look like?
- Plank—Where do things and people get their value from?

THE VALUE OF COLOSSIANS

LOCATION OF COLOSSAE
See map on page 14 for
a map of where Colossae
was.

- The Colossians _____ _____ _____, just like us.
- The Colossians _____ _____ _____ in faith, just like us.

FOUNDATION OF OUR WORLDVIEW, ACCORDING TO COLOSSIANS

- Jesus is all we need for salvation.
- God's Word is all we need for understanding.
- We are not alone on this pilgrimage. Jesus goes before us, and the Body of Christ—the Church—is all around us.

---

* The idea of describing our worldview as a raft made up of planks comes from Richard Bewes, "Could You Describe Your Worldview?" Billy Graham Evangelistic Association, January 29, 2016, https://billygraham.org/decision-magazine/february-2016/could-you-describe-your-worldview/.

The Value of Questions

- The Colossians _____ _____ _____, just like us.

The Value of People

- The Colossians wrestled _____ _____, just like us.

SEE COLOSSIANS 4:7–17.

- The Colossians also wrestled with what it means to be the _____ _____ _____ _____, just like us.

This Letter to the Colossians grounds us as individuals in a _____-centric, _____-guided, _____-driven worldview. This Letter to the Colossians also grounds the Church in a _____-centric, _____-guided, _____-driven worldview.

Discussion Questions

1. Take time to consider the planks in your raft—your worldview—today. How would you answer each of the questions I suggested as planks?
2. What are some of the factors that have influenced the planks of your worldview? Perhaps something you've been taught, something you've experienced, or relationships you've had?
3. Read the first chapter of Colossians and identify anything you hear that addresses these issues:

   Cosmology

   Christology

   Sufficiency of Christ

   Supremacy of Christ

A Special Version of Christianity?
The advanced, special Christianity that the false teachers claimed to have versus the Christianity the apostles of Jesus handed down continued to be an issue in the Early Church, even after Paul wrote to the Colossians. In fact, during the second century AD, the false teaching confronting the Colossians developed into what we know as Gnosticism.

Colossians 1:7–8
"Just as you learned it from Epaphras our beloved fellow servant. He is a faithful minister of Christ on your behalf and has made known to us your love in the Spirit."

Cosmology
The study of the beginning, or the origin, of the universe and all that is in it—including plants, continents, constellations, oceans, and people.

Christology
The study of the person, characteristics, work, and nature of Jesus Christ. Jesus is both fully God and fully a man, who walked on the earth and suffered and died for our sake.

Sufficiency
Questions of what is "enough."

Supremacy
Questions of who is in charge in the universe.

Day 1

THE FAITHFUL AND THE FAITHFUL LEADERS
COLOSSIANS 1:1–8

If I walk due east from my house, the street dead-ends into our neighborhood grocery store. During the summer months in particular, it is a favorite adventure of ours to take hiking backpacks and a wagon to procure groceries for the week. There's a strong possibility we look a bit weird, but our neighbors kindly wave and always ask after our dogs. It's the smallest small talk you can have, but it's still an encounter with our neighbors. Every time we make the grocery trek, I feel more connected and less random. I am a part of this town, this state, this place, in this giant hulking globe.

Whom do you live life connected to?

We all have family and friends we would identify as some of our close relationships. Consider the vaguer connections we have in life—the neighbor down the street, the grocery store checker, someone we go to school with, someone in the pick-up line at our children's school, or the friend of a friend who comments on our social media post. These vaguer connections are similar to what the apostle Paul had with the Colossians.

Open your Bible to Colossians 1:1–8 and note the people who are connected to this letter, whether specifically named or vaguely mentioned.

EPAPHRAS
"Just as you learned it from Epaphras our beloved fellow servant" (Colossians 1:7).

Epaphras was a pastor. He might have been the founder of the Christian congregation of Jews and Greeks in the city of Colossae in the region of Asia Minor.

LOCATION OF COLOSSAE
See page 14 for a map of Asia Minor in Paul's day.

The Colossians were friends of a friend. So why did Paul invest so much in them? Why did he send a whole letter to care for and teach and love them?

The Colossians had most likely never met Paul, but they shared an important thread of connection with Paul. It's time for some detective work. Are you ready? Colossians 1 gives us little clues about this connecting thread.

Look closely at Colossians 1:2–4. What words or phrases are repeated in both Colossians 1:2 and Colossians 1:4?

The Holy Spirit doesn't waste a word in Holy Scripture. What may seem like repetition in a simple word of greeting is actually a teaching moment from Paul's Spirit-driven pen. Let's look at each of the words Paul repeats and consider how they are more than a fancy way of saying, "Hi." Instead, these words show Paul's understanding of community.

In Christ

The phrase "in Christ" occurs frequently in Paul's writing across the New Testament. Paul actually coined the phrase. Commentators and theologians differ on exactly how many times it appears in Paul's letters, but they agree that it is central to his writings.[1] One commentator suggests there are as many as 170 occurrences of "in Christ" in Paul's letters.[2] Though the Greek phrase is translated a few different ways in our English Bibles, it is still clear that Paul used the phrase "in Christ" numerous times so that the concept would stand out to the many audiences of his Epistles.

Tiny prepositions are easy to overlook, but they can be powerful. With this little phrase, Paul captures our relationship with Christ as an ongoing relationship. At the moment of our Baptism, we are placed "in Christ," and we receive His righteousness. The righteousness we have at the beginning of our relationship with Christ continues to be ours in this moment and in tomorrow's moments too. When God looks on us, He sees us "in Christ" and therefore our judgment from God is righteousness and holiness, rather than sin and separation. The most important thing that could be true of us is that we are "in Christ." It's so important, Paul makes a point to start his letter by describing the Colossians as those who are "in Christ." Praise God, because this is true for us as well! "In Christ" is our very identity.

This little phrase also reminds us that our God wants to spend time with us, just as we are, and can spend time with us, just as we are, because Christ's redemptive work is *in* us, not only placed on us, or done for us. Regularly we get to meet with Him, hear His Word, and sit at His table because we are "in Christ." "In Christ" reflects the protection and ongoing care God pours out on His people—including the Colossian believers and us.

What do you think the significance of being "in Christ" is, as opposed to being by, on, with, or through Christ?

COMMUNITY
A group of people living life together, whether because of close proximity, mutual interests, or other common bonds. In this book, I reserve the word *community* for the goal and process of genuine life together, rather than a vague idea of locality or grouping. Genuine community is living life together in authenticity—where accountability and individual gifts are valued, but also where mistakes, forgiveness, and grace are understood as necessary. In genuine life together, growth is valued over perfection. This meaning of *community* is the goal, however imperfect our experience of it might be.

EPISTLE
A fancy word for "letter"; a handwritten note used to communicate information and thoughts.

"In Christ" makes the two other connecting terms in Colossians 1:2 and 1:4 possible.

Faith/Faithful

SEEING THE MYSTERY
In 1 Timothy 3:9, Paul specifically calls faith a mystery.

Faith is the connecting glue of God's people. The words *faith* and *faithful* are related. We receive faith as a gift at the moment of our Baptism, and then, as we live the rest of our lives in that Baptism, we are full of faith, or *faithful*. It's a mighty, mysterious, and wonderful thing. Paul, Timothy, and the Colossians have a shared life because they share the same faith, the same grounding perspective. The connection of the life they share in faith gives Paul and Timothy credibility with the Colossians and gives validity to their writing and care for the Colossians.

PSALM 56:8
"You have kept count of my tossings; put my tears in Your bottle. Are they not in Your book?"

Faith in God changes everything in a believer's life. It changed everything for the Colossians and it changes everything for us. Faith is abstract, but it affects our lives physically, mentally, and emotionally every day. We can be going about our business unaware of God's presence and action. Then we hear an encouraging Word at just the right time. When we are sad, we are comforted with the promise that God collects our tears. Our family relationships, our friendships, and all our relationships with others can be imperfect and frustrating at times, but faith helps us realize that they are not accidental. God is working His connecting purpose into them, and by faith, we see glimpses of that.

Because faith is abstract, it can also be confusing. Part of the purpose of the Letter to the Colossians was to give that group of believers long ago a stronger grounding in their faith. I don't know about you, but I need firmer grounding in my faith every day! The slush of life can be confusing, and I need help applying the abstract truths and realities of our faith to my concrete situations.

Let's take a moment to connect abstract faith to everyday life. For each of the following Bible verses, identify a characteristic of faith described in the passage, and then brainstorm how that characteristic impacts our day-to-day lives.

	Characteristic	Impact
Hebrews 11:1		
Romans 10:17		
1 Thessalonians 1:2–3		
1 John 5:4		

Saints/Brothers

The other word repeated in Colossians 1:2 and 1:4 is *saints*. *Saints* sounds like a fancy-dancy church word. But there's a reason Paul calls those in Colossae *brothers* as well as *saints* in Colossians 1:2. In Christ, the words *brothers* and *saints* are connected. They actually create connection between us when we speak them to one another. They show that God works in families; but His definition of family is much wider than our own.

According to Luke 8:21, whom does Jesus count as brothers?

You are in God's family as a hearer of His Word and disciple of His grace.

Relationships between family members aren't easily cut off. Even when family members are estranged, they are still oddly and mysteriously connected. We can't fully shake our connections with those we're related to, even if we want to. So it is within the Body of Christ. By using the word *brothers*, Paul and Timothy lay groundwork for the Colossians to see themselves as being closely connected to Paul and Timothy, even though they have never met one another.

In the category of weird but true, sainthood is not too far removed from the concept of family. We might think of Mother Teresa when we hear the word *saint*, or maybe we think of St. Paul or St. Timothy. But the Greek word for *saints* in Colossians 1:2, *hagiois*, is simply associated with being set apart or holy. Saints are those who are linked to the nature of Christ instead of the nature of the world.[3] Because we are in Christ, when God looks at us, He sees even our messiness through a Jesus lens. He sees our story whole and complete in Jesus. He sees us as saints. This status connects us to Him in a way that is not true of nonbelievers. Sainthood (and brotherhood, for that matter) isn't about how special we are. It's about the gift of God, connecting us to Himself.

Reread Colossians 1:1. What does Paul say about Timothy in this verse?

Even the authorship of the Letter to the Colossians gives a nod to the ways God mysteriously and mightily connects us. Paul notes a coauthor in many of his epistles, though not all of them. In many cases, this coauthor is Timothy. If you are curious, look up the introduction to each Pauline Epistle, listed in the sidebar. Some commentators say Timothy is often listed as a coauthor because Paul needed a scribe to assist him. However, there may be more to Timothy's role in writing these New Testament Epistles alongside

---

BODY OF CHRIST
A uniquely descriptive and biblical phrase for the Church. This phrase refers to the people of God, knit together by His Spirit, with Jesus Christ as the head of the Body. Through this image, God gives us a picture of how the Church grows—intimately connected to the head, Jesus—and how it functions as a united Body made up of a diverse group of members. Jesus is the intimate connection and connector of all of us who are in the Church.

ἀδελφοῖς
adelphois: brothers, or brothers and sisters.

This term can be used for blood relatives, such as siblings, as well as other close, though not biological, relationships. Can you hear the closeness implied by speaking of friends as if they had come from the same womb, as siblings do?[16]

COAUTHORS IN PAUL'S EPISTLES
Find the coauthors of the Pauline Epistles mentioned in these verses:

1 Corinthians 1:1

Galatians 1:1–2

Philippians 1:1

2 Corinthians 1:1

1 Thessalonians 1:1

2 Thessalonians 1:1

Philemon 1

Paul. We call this an open question,[4] which means we aren't sure of the answer. It's important that we are honest when we don't know something for sure, especially when studying the Bible. Maybe Timothy is mentioned at the beginning of Colossians because Paul had a mentor relationship with this young pastor; maybe Timothy had special insight into the Colossian crew in particular. What exactly Timothy did or did not do in writing Colossians is something we probably won't know till we see our Savior face-to-face. But I tend to wonder if Paul purposefully mentioned Timothy and wrote as "we" instead of "I" to bring the "we" of faith to the Colossian believers' attention. This concept of "we" continues to be one of the hardest parts of faith for us to wrap our heads around.

THE WE OF COMMUNITY

These opening words to the Colossians are steeped in connection and community in more ways than I can count!

Read Colossians 1:3–4 again below and circle every *we* you can find.

We always thank God, the Father of our Lord Jesus Christ, when we pray for you, since we heard of your faith in Christ Jesus and of the love that you have for all the saints. (Colossians 1:3–4)

We thank. *We* pray. *We* heard. Again, small words make a big difference. The *we*'s in these verses are also the *we*'s of leadership. Paul has authority as an "apostle of Christ Jesus" and "by the will of God" (1:1). However, what makes the authority really stick is the relationship between the people involved. Connection in Christ and the community He creates bind Paul and God, bind Paul and Timothy, bind the Colossians together, and bind Paul and Timothy and the Colossians to one another. It is only where there is community that people can hear and take to heart admonitions and exhortations like those God gave through Paul to the Colossians in the rest of this letter.

CONNECTION + AUTHORITY = LEADERSHIP

People have a hard time listening to leaders because we're all sinners—both the leaders and the hearers. Leaders are broken people trying to help other broken people. If the equation for leadership doesn't include connection, there is only authority; and people will only listen for so long to someone who has authority over them but no connection to them. Without authority, there is only connection in the equation, and the result is confusion about who to listen to. Then we end up where the Colossians ended up, listening to the wisdom of people who are leading away from the Gospel, listening to demands for special knowledge or ideas God never invented. Very early in the opening of his letter, Paul not only reminds the Colossians of his connection to and authority toward them, but he also points the Colossians to another leader who embodies the whole equation, who has a personal connection with them and authority: Epaphras.

What designations does Paul give Epaphras in Colossians 1:7–8?

Whom do you consider to be a faithful leader in the Christian Church at large? How do they connect to the people of local churches?

Whom do you consider to be a faithful leader in your local church? How do they connect to you and other people?

We as faithful (faith-filled) people need faithful (faith-filled) leaders. And we need to listen to, converse with, and question these faithful leaders in genuine relationships, connected in genuine community. We are a messy bunch of believers in the Body of Christ. You'll find out throughout our study that the Colossians were also a messy bunch of believers in the Body of Christ. But God is faithful—always—even when we are not. And He lovingly raises up all around us faithful, while imperfect, leaders. Leadership, authority, and connection are all complicated. But the gift of being connected to one another makes the complications worth the trouble.

We are connected closer than we know by a Savior who has all authority over our lives and our hearts. He holds us close to Himself and one another in mighty faith, mighty hope, and mighty love.

Connected by His Word

Use the Scripture memory verse for the week and the prayer prompt to bring your confession, thanksgiving, praise, and requests before our mighty and mysterious God.

CHURCH LEADERSHIP
God sends leaders for our benefit. For example, God chose Moses to be the leader of the Israelites as God brought them out of Egypt and to the Promised Land (see Exodus 4). Can you imagine the Israelites leaving Egypt and making it through forty years in the wilderness without a leader who pointed them to God's faithfulness over and over again?

When our leaders are imperfect, it can be difficult for us to remember that God is the one who put them in their position of leadership—and that He did so for our good. By nature, we prefer the *I* of our own ideas instead of the *we* of community. Faithful leaders point us to God's Word, to God's gifts, and to one another, working to the best of their ability for the best interest of the whole community. Faithful leaders will fail at times. But that doesn't mean we don't need leaders in the Church, nor does it mean God made a mistake in choosing our leaders. Instead, at those times, it's our turn to point our leaders to God's faithfulness and His grace and forgiveness.

Week 1 Memory Verse

Since we heard of your faith in Christ Jesus and of the love that you have for all the saints. (Colossians 1:4)

Prayer Prompt

Lord, You are faithful when people—including me—are not. Guide Your people to reflect Your faithfulness today . . .

When You Pray . . .

If you're not sure what to pray, here is a potential outline for your prayers. But this is your prayer time, so feel free to think outside of these categories— use some, don't use others, and add whatever you like.

Confession—Presenting our guilt before God: broadly, that we are sinners, or narrowly, by admitting and presenting specific sins for Him to heal and forgive.

Thanksgiving—Offering our gratitude before God, through the Holy Spirit, for all that He has done for us and gives to us.

Praise—Recognizing God for who He is, such as Creator, Redeemer, Restorer, Defender, and so forth.

Requests—Sharing with God what needs you have, asking for help, seeking guidance, recognizing His hand in your life and in the lives of those around you.

Day 2

FRUITFUL TREES AND CHURCH PLANTING
COLOSSIANS 1:3–8

When my husband and I were in college, we each had to write a paper about a church community who had made a difference in our lives. The thing I remember most about this assignment was that the congregation my husband wrote about was only about fourteen years old! I had never considered that churches begin as fresh young things . . . just as adults start as tiny babies. In my young adult mind, I thought congregations had always been around, as if created out of nothing or grown in the Garden of Eden or something. But in reality, there was once a day when each church on this earth didn't exist, and then a few someones, by their sweat and tears, created a living, breathing congregation.

What do you imagine the beginnings of a church look like? What kinds of things go into the start of a church community?

What faith beginnings have you been part of? (E.g., Baptism, moving and finding a new church, becoming involved with a new Christian organization)

God *can* do the work of His kingdom out of thin air and burning bushes, but He almost always chooses to do His work through people—people like Paul, Timothy, Epaphras, the Colossians, you, and me. I now know that just as people are planted in a certain time and place for God's work, so also churches are planted by God in particular times and places.

We often call the work of God *fruit* (like "fruit of the Spirit," Galatians 5:22). Fruit and planting are closely related.

Open your Bible to Colossians 1:1–8 and note any language connected to fruit and planting in the passage:

Isaiah 55:10–11
"For as the rain and the snow come down from heaven and do not return there but water the earth, making it bring forth and sprout, giving seed to the sower and bread to the eater, so shall My word be that goes out from My mouth; it shall not return to Me empty, but it shall accomplish that which I purpose, and shall succeed in the thing for which I sent it."

These verses show that the Gospel has power: when it is heard, it produces fruit. God promises elsewhere that His Word does not go out and come back to Him void and empty. This means we are free to stop looking at our lives, trying so hard to see fruit; instead, God invites us to place our focus where He promises to give fruit: His Word.

Look at Colossians 1:5–6 specifically and fill in the blanks below:

Of this you have heard before in the _____ _____ _____, the gospel, which has _____ _____ _____, as indeed in the whole world it is bearing fruit and increasing—as it also does _____ _____, since the day you heard it and understood the grace of God in truth.

THE WORD OF TRUTH . . .
COME TO YOU

God puts His Spirit into us when we are baptized and He sends us out into this world. Each of our testimonies of how He brought us to Himself looks different, but His faithfulness in finding us, coming to us, is the same. Paul, Timothy, and Epaphras each had their own stories that witnessed to how God's Word came to them and bore fruit. Their stories are each encouraging in different ways.

What uniqueness do you see in each of these men's lives? How did God bring His Spirit and Word to each of them? What fruit do you see mentioned in these passages?

Paul—Acts 9:1–19

Timothy—2 Timothy 1:1–7

We don't know very much about Epaphras, do we? He is mentioned again later in Colossians and in Philemon 23. We'll talk about his story more in week 6 of our study. For now, it's enough to know that Epaphras was the connecting piece between Paul and the Colossians. Commentators suggest perhaps Epaphras came to Paul in prison, asking for help because the Church in Colossae was struggling.[5] Paul and Timothy then wrote this Letter to the Colossians to address some of Epaphras's concerns and to support him as he cared for the Colossian Church community. Though Epaphras seems to have been a prominent leader in Colossae, he wasn't alone. God placed people in his life who could help him, and he was willing to ask for help when troubles in Colossae began.

Paul and Timothy also needed and had help from other Christians. Paul had Ananias; Timothy had Lois and Eunice. We need one another too. God faithfully places people in our lives who can support us when trouble comes. We are not alone. So much fruit can come from working together and asking for help!

Our stories of God's Word coming to us and finding us are touched again and again by people. How did God initially bring His Word into your life? Who were the people He used to share it with you?

Whom has God used to help and guide you when you most needed it?

> **COLOSSIANS 4:12–13**
> "Epaphras, who is one of you, a servant of Christ Jesus, greets you, always struggling on your behalf in his prayers, that you may stand mature and fully assured in all the will of God. For I bear him witness that he has worked hard for you and for those in Laodicea and in Hierapolis."

> **ACTS 9:17**
> "So Ananias departed and entered the house. And laying his hands on him he said, 'Brother Saul, the Lord Jesus who appeared to you on the road by which you came has sent me so that you may regain your sight and be filled with the Holy Spirit.'"

> **2 TIMOTHY 1:5**
> "I am reminded of your sincere faith, a faith that dwelt first in your grandmother Lois and your mother Eunice and now, I am sure, dwells in you as well."

THE WORD OF TRUTH . . .
AMONG YOU

Paul says the Word of truth is bearing fruit and increasing in the whole world and among the Colossians. But as we already know, that did not mean the Colossians did not have their share of problems. Sometimes we see more evidence of our weakness than evidence that God's Word is bearing fruit in us and among us. Yet Paul does not seem discouraged or dissuaded by the weakness he knows exists among the Colossians. Instead, Paul knew that God promises to do His work even in spite of our weakness—and in fact that God does His best work in the midst of our weakness.

Read 2 Corinthians 12:5–10. What lesson did Paul learn in his life and ministry about God's faithfulness and human weaknesses?

What weaknesses have been part of your life? How have these weaknesses impacted your relationship with God?

Turn to 1 Corinthians 12:22–27. Here Paul talks about the complexity of the Body of Christ. How do weaknesses work in the Body of Christ?

What "weaknesses" can you identify in your local church community?

God's Word comes to us and works among us in the midst of every single one of these weaknesses. Experiencing our weaknesses *together* is an essential part of experiencing life together as one Body:

If one member suffers, all suffer together; if one member is honored, all rejoice together.
(1 Corinthians 12:26)

Circle the words *one* and *all* in the verse above. So often we feel like *one*. I am pretty confident that Paul, Timothy, and Epaphras also sometimes felt the struggle of being *one*; but they knew God's faithfulness in using His Word to move His people from *one* to *all*.

Colossians 1:4–5 gives clues about what it looks like when we move from *one* to *all* in our lives and churches. What three fruits did Epaphras report to Paul and Timothy as results of the Word being among the Colossians?

Since we heard of your _____ (v. 4)

and of the _____ that you have (v. 4)

because of the _____ laid up for you (v. 5)

God is the one who works faith, hope, and love into our lives. When we hear from God's Word of Christ's willingness to sacrifice Himself and rise that first Easter long ago to give us new life, then faith, hope, and love are cultivated in us, and they work mysteriously among us. We also hear in God's Word of the Spirit's constant presence with us, bringing fruit and more fruit—more faith, more love, more hope. By the Spirit's power, we stand firm in our faith together. We suffer and rejoice together, loving one another even when relationships are hard, when they're exhausting, and when we'd rather ditch out. We share hope when one or many of us feel hopeless. We remind one another that Jesus is coming back for us one day; therefore, death and our struggles that *feel* like death are not the end of our stories. As we wait for Him to return, we also remind one another that Jesus is the one who brings the increasing in our faith, hope, and love, and He is the one who gives grace and more grace. The world terribly needs the fruit that only Jesus can give. May His fruit be present in and go out from each one of us and from *all* of us each day.

Connected by the Word

Use the Scripture memory verse for the week and the prayer prompt to bring your confession, thanksgiving, praise, and requests before our mighty and mysterious God.

Week 1 Memory Verse

Since we heard of your faith in Christ Jesus and of the love that you have for all the saints. (Colossians 1:4)

Prayer Prompt

Father, You give faith, love, and hope in abundance through Your Son and Your Spirit. Be with those I know who are suffering and those who are rejoicing . . .

1 Corinthians 13:13
"So now faith, hope, and love abide, these three; but the greatest of these is love."

Author's Note
Our faith, hope, and love often waver. People can and will give only imperfect expressions of these. But God gives hope that will never fail us, even when we feel hopeless. His love is 100 percent sure and true. He loves us without conditions, and He is the same today as He was yesterday and will be tomorrow. God is always and completely faithful.

Day 3

Communication is complicated, and yet most of us communicate with people constantly. One communication technique that can be useful is known as "the feedback sandwich." I'm not sure where this method originated, but the general principle of the feedback sandwich is this: when you need to tell someone constructive criticism, you sandwich it between statements of positive affirmation. The idea is that it's easier to hear criticism in this way, rather than being blasted by someone's criticism. This technique can certainly be helpful for communication with family members, roommates, or anyone else who breathes the same air we do.

But the feedback sandwich is also hotly debated. Is it manipulative? Are the praise parts of the feedback sandwich actually genuine? And does the praise really matter if you tuck criticism in the middle of it? Every theory and technique in life has holes and can be misapplied. There is no one right way to communicate in every situation.

What have you found enables you to hear and receive constructive criticism from others?

I read an article once that said constructive feedback is better described as a wrap than a sandwich.[6] Wrapping is exactly how I would describe Paul's approach in his Letter to the Colossians. He begins this letter by talking about his authority—he is an apostle by God's will—and about the relationship he has with the recipients of the letter—they are his brothers and sisters, saints in the same Christ, followers of the same God. He does this so that they understand that he is the same as them before God, even while he has been appointed to speak to them on God's behalf. Paul again highlights the relationship the readers of the letter have with the whole Body of Christ at the end of Colossians. Yet Paul also teaches about God's authority and human relationships in the Body of Christ throughout the letter. Therefore, Paul wraps, rather than sandwiches, his Letter to the Colossians in the overarching theological points he wants them to learn.

Remember, it is likely that Paul had never met the Colossians in person. It's easy to think people would of course just listen to the apostle Paul, because ... well ... he's *the apostle Paul*.

I'm not sure it works that way though.

Paul does state in the first verse of his letter that he has authority as an apostle by God's will; yet Paul understood that we don't listen to our teachers simply because they are teachers or to our parents simply because they are parents. More often, we listen and heed the words of those in authority over us because of the relationship we have with them, the concern and affection they have shown for us.

Remember the equation from day 1?

CONNECTION + AUTHORITY= LEADERSHIP

Has anyone ever given you unsolicited advice? Was it someone with whom you had only a vague relationship or no relationship at all? What did this advice-giving experience look like? What emotions did it bring up for you?

Paul and Timothy, knowing all of this about the tenderness of authority and relationship, right away at the beginning of their letter speak of their spiritual care for and investment in the Colossians. This is not fake emotional manipulation or buttering up. Paul and Timothy love the Colossians as members of the same Body, children of the same heavenly Father, bound together by the same Savior.

Read through Colossians 1:1–11. Which words and actions show that Paul and Timothy are authentically walking alongside the Colossians, rather than simply sharing an opinion or talking at them?

Prayer changes relationships. Prayer creates a level of intimacy in relationships that is different from anything the world could ever offer us. This kind of intimacy can only be created by the mysterious working of our connecting God.

Paul's words to the Colossians are more than, "Hey, I'm praying for you! Peace out," with no follow-through. The Greek phrase in Colossians 1:9 translated as, "We have not ceased to pray for you," more literally could be translated, "We are not stopping praying and asking for you."[7]

οὐ παυόμεθα
ou pauometha: we are not stopping

προσευχόμενοι
proseuchomenoi: praying, offering petitions (requests) to God[17]

αἰτούμενοι
aitoumenoi: asking, requesting[18]

Can you hear the ongoing investment in the literal translation, with its *-ing*s? "We can't stop. We won't stop. We must pray for you. We will keep praying for you." These small nuances reflect the authentic care Paul and Timothy show for the Colossians, even in Paul's and Timothy's daily habits. The first step in praying for someone is thinking of that someone. Prayer is always a Spirit-driven action. God is the one who brings people to our minds and grows our relationships by prompting us to pray for others.

I'm reminded of my husband's grandmother. Grandma Fabis was a pray-er. It wasn't uncommon to find a note from her in the mailbox once every few weeks, giving you tidbits of news and a reminder you had been prayed for. One summer, we went to Guatemala for a week to serve and support full-time missionaries. We asked Grandma to be our prayer partner. I had no idea how seriously she took this job until a few years after our travels, she showed me her prayer log. In this log, she recorded whom she prayed for and when each day. During our time in Guatemala, she had prayed for us no less than thirty times in a single day.

Grandma Fabis's prayers were her first gift to us. When she told us that she had been praying for us, she gave us a second gift: our relationship with her was strengthened by her prayers. This is exactly what Paul and Timothy are doing in Colossians 1:9–11.

Read Colossians 1:9–11 below, and underline each request Paul and Timothy report presenting on the Colossians' behalf.

And so, from the day we heard, we have not ceased to pray for you, asking that you may be filled with the knowledge of His will in all spiritual wisdom and understanding, so as to walk in a manner worthy of the Lord, fully pleasing to Him: bearing fruit in every good work and increasing in the knowledge of God; being strengthened with all power, according to His glorious might, for all endurance and patience with joy. (Colossians 1:9–11)

Let's learn from each of these requests by listing them in bullet points. These are all things the Colossians needed in their context, but they are certainly also things we need in our own time and place as well.

⊞ Spiritual Wisdom, Understanding, and Walking the Walk

Faith comes by hearing the Word of God. The Colossians were being led by false teachers in their midst down a slippery slope of "you should, you must do x, y, or z to truly be a Christian." These false teachers told them they needed particular rituals and special knowledge in order to be connected to God—something beyond what God had said in His Word.

ROMANS 10:17
"Faith comes from hearing, and hearing through the word of Christ."

Paul and Timothy again and again will affirm for the Colossians that the knowledge of Jesus Christ alone, coupled with faith, is always enough for salvation. That sounds simple, but this is where spiritual wisdom and understanding come in. Spiritual understanding is the understanding brought by *faith*, rather than information. In all the circumstances of life, spiritual wisdom says Jesus alone is enough for the salvation of all people. Spiritual understanding says Jesus alone is enough for *my* salvation! Wisdom changes the head, and understanding changes the heart as well as the walk a person is walking. We can't give ourselves wisdom or understanding any more than we can make the sun rise. But that is why Paul and Timothy pray for the Colossians to receive these gifts from God—because God is faithful to make us wise and give us understanding and insight, opening our blind eyes and our deaf ears to His Word.

Opening the Bible, as you're doing right now in this study, and going to church to hear God's Word are always the best ways for knowledge, wisdom, understanding, and the fruits of faith to grow. The Word keeps our legs moving on this spiritual journey, even when they get weary carrying the stuff of life.

What Scripture verses, stories, or passages have jumped out at you recently and been encouraging in your daily walk?

⊩—⊩ Strength, Endurance, and Patience

My head hurts anytime I'm part of a conversation about the vastness of God or one that attempts to understand His thoughts and ways. Don't get me wrong, I enjoy it! But it is mentally taxing in a way that making dinner or returning emails is not. It is hard enough to comprehend what God says about His bigness, but then we also hear, read, or see the untruths that people come up with about God. We know that the Colossians, just like each of us, heard a thousand different messages about God from a hundred different angles. This has been true in any time and place and will continue to be true until Jesus comes again. Notice how Paul and Timothy responded to this problem: They didn't tell the Colossians to live in a commune and avoid external contact. Instead, Paul and Timothy prayed for the Colossians' strength.

What kind of strength did these leaders pray over the people in Colossians 1:11?

This Bible study isn't called *The Mighty and the Mysterious* for nothing. We have a powerful God. We have a glorious God. We have a mighty God.

Flip through the pages of your Bible and recall what big, mighty acts God has done. These have been recorded so we can return to them and remember His might when we need strength. List three of those big, mighty acts to help them stick in your heart and mind today.

God is also full of an everyday kind of might. There are angels guarding and keeping us while we drive around town or sleep in our beds. I'm also thinking of the might our God gives us when we need the courage to walk into a situation with a difficult family member, the guts to have the sex talk with our adolescent child, or the right words at the right time and place, though we may stumble over them imperfectly.

What small, everyday mighty acts have you seen God do in your life and home?

Paul and Timothy also pray for the Colossians to have endurance. Commentators define *endurance* as "patience coupled with restraint." The Colossians' lives were complicated. Our lives are complicated. People are complicated. Endurance isn't the act of doing all things well and all things turning out the way we'd like in the end. Rather, endurance is God-given and God-driven. It is the act of walking through the valley and the desert when we'd rather be on the mountaintop. Sometimes it is keeping our mouths closed when we'd rather speak. Sometimes it is staying put when we'd rather run. Only our mighty God can enable us to do those things. Therefore, we powerfully reflect Him to the world when we live like that.

That's why Paul and Timothy pray for the Colossians to have endurance, as well as patience *to* endure. Patience is letting God do His work in our lives when life throws us curveballs—accepting and tolerating the circumstances He sends that seem less than desirable to us because we trust Him to do what is best. It seems to me that endurance is the acting out of that patient restraint. It is not throwing the big fit, not spewing the words of hurt, not giving up; it is asking for help, opening the Word when we are disappointed, crying out to God in our weariness. Because these things are so difficult to do and they go against all of our instincts, patience and endurance are some of the trademarks of those who are in Christ: only God causes them to grow in our lives.

😄 With Joy

In the Bible, the concepts of joy and endurance are both commonly connected to the idea of long-suffering.

Oh goody.

Take a peek at the following verses and see for yourself. How are joy, long-suffering, and endurance connected in each passage?

Ezra 3:11–13

Romans 12:12

James 1:2–3

Sometimes life is really hard, and it seems nearly impossible to feel joy. We do not need to plaster on a fake smile and pretend to have joy in the middle of our sorrow. Nowhere in the Bible does God tell someone, "Please don't tell Me what you're actually thinking and feeling. I'd rather you just pretend with Me." However, when we talk about joy in Scripture, it's helpful to think about it as Joy with a capital *J*. It is a supernatural gift of God, related to His might and glory. Joy in the Book of Colossians and the rest of the Bible is the result of God showing His favor—it is undeserved and unrelated to our circumstances. Rather, it exists because of His faithfulness.

Joy, connected to long-suffering and endurance, is also connected to sacrifice—because it is connected to Christ. Paul and Timothy knew tribulation as well as Joy. Paul knew painful prayers, cried out from his prison cell, for people miles and miles away in Colossae. But he and Timothy knew the work of God's Spirit in the middle of this mess of life, not in spite of it. And as a result, they knew just how powerful God's strength is and how much God lavishes when He gives spiritual wisdom, understanding, endurance, and patience.

So at the end of the day, Paul's heartfelt message to the Colossians in Colossians 1:9–11 is this:

PRAYING YOU THROUGH, COLOSSIANS. PRAYING YOU THROUGH.

What is God doing, and where is God working in our lives? Sometimes we're not sure, and often we won't know. I hope you are blessed to have someone in your life praying for you in the way Paul prayed for the Colossians. But whether you do or don't, you can rest in the promise that you have a mighty Savior who is interceding for you. He is praying you through.

Write out Romans 8:34 in the space below or, better yet, put it on a notecard or a sticky note in a place you will often see it. Let it remind you of the Joy found in your mighty Savior, the one who prays you through.

CONNECTED BY THE WORD

Use the Scripture memory verse for the week and the prayer prompt to bring your confession, thanksgiving, praise, and requests before our mighty and mysterious God.

WEEK 1 MEMORY VERSE

Since we heard of your faith in Christ Jesus and of the love that you have for all the saints. (Colossians 1:4)

PRAYER PROMPT

Christ Jesus, thank You for interceding for me every day in every way. Today I pray for the strength of Your might and Your beautiful Joy over . . .

Day 4

A SHARED INHERITANCE
COLOSSIANS 1:12

I have an extreme dislike for the thumbs-up emoji. I'm grateful for relationships that are solid enough to handle weird idiosyncrasies, because this is certainly one of mine. You never really understand how badly something bothers you until you lose it regarding that thing during a random conversation, and everyone looks at you as though you have two heads. Thankfully, my extremism regarding the thumbs-up emoji manifested itself during a texting conversation with my sisters, rather than with someone else. While planning an upcoming family visit, our conversation looked something like this:

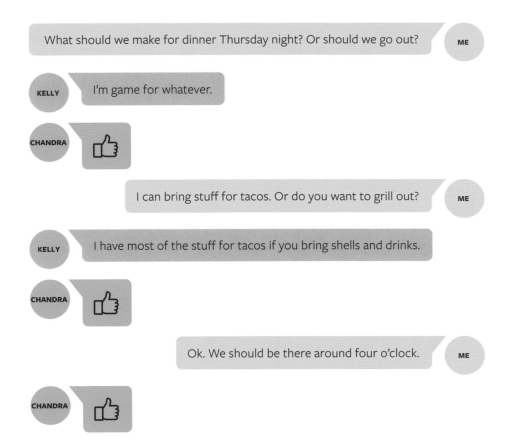

What should we make for dinner Thursday night? Or should we go out? **ME**

KELLY I'm game for whatever.

CHANDRA 👍

I can bring stuff for tacos. Or do you want to grill out? **ME**

KELLY I have most of the stuff for tacos if you bring shells and drinks.

CHANDRA 👍

Ok. We should be there around four o'clock. **ME**

CHANDRA 👍

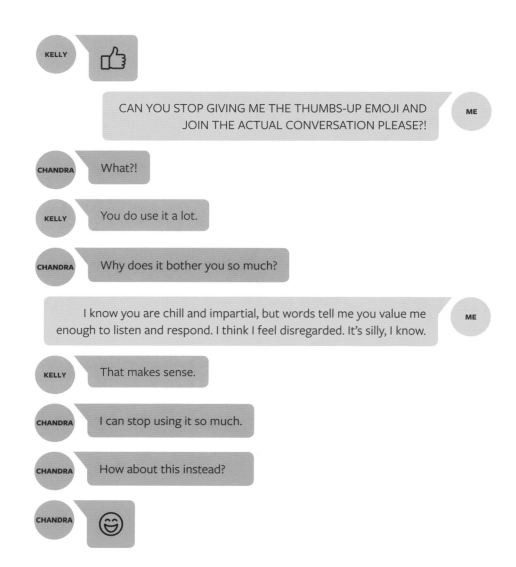

My sisters have a good sense of humor and are usually willing to humor me—weird idiosyncrasies and all. It's not that I don't appreciate the convenience of the thumbs-up emoji. It quickly communicates, "I've got you. We're good. This plan is solid. Whatever you say. We're good to go."

However, this world often lacks affirmation. We need to hear and to express value and thankfulness in every space we can.

What in life makes you feel like I do when I receive a thumbs-up emoji?

What small habits or idiosyncrasies do you have that rob your focus and leave you forgetting to speak value over someone?

Paul regularly declared value over people, sharing his gratitude for their existence and for the life he shared with them in the Body.

In each of the following verses, whom does Paul give thanks for?

1 Corinthians 1:4

Philippians 1:3–5

2 Thessalonians 1:3

1 Timothy 2:1

What people might you add to your list of praise and thanksgiving offered before God?

Prayer and thanksgiving seem to go hand in hand for Paul and Timothy. They begin in Colossians 1:3 by saying, "We always thank God . . . when we pray for you." In the rest of Colossians 1, we see them pray that the Colossians would have spiritual wisdom and understanding, that they would walk in a way that pleases the Lord, that they would bear fruit, and that they would be strengthened with God's power. And then Paul and Timothy pray that the Colossians themselves would also be thankful.

Turn the pages of your Bible back to Colossians 1:9–12. Read the passage. Then write Colossians 1:12 in the space below. Let this exercise help focus your thoughts today on this particular verse.

What does Paul say in Colossians 1:12 is a reason for the Colossians to give thanks to the Father?

Paul and Timothy remind the Colossians they have been qualified before God, redeemed through Jesus' work on the cross and His resurrection over the grave. God has made them qualified. There is nothing left for them to do. They are enough.

Think of how powerful that would have been in the Colossians' context: They had false teachers among them who were saying things like, "You're not enough yet. You're not doing enough. You don't know enough. You're not enough."

So how does Paul respond? He tells them, "You are enough. *In Christ.*"

What is devaluing about the message "You are not enough"? When you say those words out loud to yourself, what emotions come to the surface?

No matter if we are six weeks old in the womb or 108 years old, we need to hear the Word of God and be reminded that Jesus Christ has been absolutely enough on our behalf and that He makes us absolutely enough. Our value is found in whom we belong to, not what we know or how well we perform. The message of "Jesus is enough" is so vital, so central to Scripture that we could flip to any book of the Bible and find assurance there of God the Father sending God the Son as the Savior to qualify us and God the Spirit proclaiming over us:

IN CHRIST, YOU ARE ENOUGH.

We live in a world full of thumbs-up emojis. We also live in a world of "Do more, be better, you don't know enough." We need to hear truth over and over again. Listen to these words. They are true for you, as they were true for the Colossians: in Christ, you are enough.

It's spiritually and emotionally grounding to remember the truth:

WE ARE ENOUGH IN CHRIST.

Paul gives thanks for the Colossians because of who they are in connection to Christ. They are Paul's fellow saints and his brothers and sisters. They are in Christ with him—together. Then here, in Colossians 1:12, Paul prays they will give thanks for one another for the same reason: they share an identity; they have been qualified by God, they are enough in Christ. This is the foundation of their relationships as believers, and it informs their worldview as they share life together. It is exactly the same for us.

We see Paul describe this shared identity in a number of ways in the New Testament.

What language of being qualified and being enough can you find in the following passages from Paul's letters?

2 Corinthians 3:4–6

Romans 8:1–4

Galatians 3:26–27

Galatians says we are sons of God in Christ Jesus. This connects to what Colossians says about our inheritance. In Christ, we receive an inheritance that comes from being God's sons and daughters. If we have been made God's children, we have a closer relationship with Him than if we had simply been called His "followers." In God's family, we don't have to hide parts of ourselves—neither our bumps, bruises, and scars, nor our abilities—because our inheritance depends on Jesus, not on us. God's family inheritance in Christ gives us hope, purpose, identity, forgiveness.

The fact that this inheritance is shared—that all of us in God's family have this inheritance—can be hard for us to swallow sometimes. We live in a "me first" culture, and let's face it: our sinful selves want to be the most special of all the special people. Sometimes we don't want someone else to be qualified for this inheritance. Sometimes we look at our skills and abilities or our successes and we think we should be more or less qualified for this inheritance than someone else. And yet God gave us a gift when He gave us one another through this shared inheritance. When we look at life around us with confusion and concern, we are not alone. The discernment and understanding that are part of our inheritance in Christ are not easy to put into practice. But we are not alone. We live in a family of believers.

What are some of the ways other people walking with Jesus, other inheritors of "enough," shine light into our lives?

The promises of God have an exponential effect among us when we see them as real, working acts of the Holy Spirit not only in our lives, but also in one another's lives. Because that is true, we study God's Word *together*, praying for God to give us knowledge and understanding *together*. We support one another as we ask hard questions *together* about the teaching we hear and wrestle to discern what aligns with the Word of truth.

The King James translation's word choice in Colossians 1:12 helps us think of how we also share in this inheritance together in a very physical, tangible way:

Giving thanks unto the Father, which hath made us meet to be partakers of the inheritance of the saints in light. (Colossians 1:12, KJV)

Being a partaker means we get to join in and be a part of things; we aren't left out in the cold. But *partake* can also mean joining in eating or drinking, having a portion of a meal that is shared.

Where is one place we gather as children with an inheritance, according to Luke 22:18–20?

THE LORD'S SUPPER
In 1 Corinthians 11:23–25, Paul reminds the Corinthian Christians of these words from Luke 22:18–20 that Jesus spoke at His Last Supper. Churches everywhere continue to repeat these words—called the Words of Institution for the Lord's Supper—when they share this Sacrament together.

Invited together around God's table is a fellowship the world can't give. The Holy Spirit, through God's Word, knits believers together:

- We hold one another up when we feel less than qualified.

- We share the Word. We share our lives. We share mercy, when the world is a harsh place to be.

- We ground our identity in this glorious and mighty inheritance that we receive through God the Son.

- We stand as saints—together. Reminding one another we are worthy of more than simple thumbs-up emojis.

- We shine the light of truth into one another's darkness when the world envelops us in falsehood.

Qualified and worthy together: friends, family, fellow saints.

Connected by the Word

Use the Scripture memory verse for the week and the prayer prompt to bring your confession, thanksgiving, praise, and requests before our mighty and mysterious God.

Week 1 Memory Verse

Since we heard of your faith in Christ Jesus and of the love that you have for all the saints. (Colossians 1:4)

Prayer Prompt

Savior, I am not worthy of Your inheritance, but You died so that I can receive this inheritance and be a brother, a sister, in Your Father's household. Help me to claim this identity today . . .

Day 5

DARK AND LIGHT, AND LIFE WITHOUT THE CHURCH
COLOSSIANS 1:12–14

Very often the world screams of darkness.

It seems to hit us like a semi-truck at some point in adulthood, but it creeps into childhood sooner than we'd like.

- school shootings
- divorce in families
- gossip all around us—finding out it's about us
- cancer, loss

What were some of the dark things of the world that you first became aware of as a child?

What dark and difficult things dawned on you later, as an adult?

JOHN 1:5
"The light shines in the darkness, and the darkness has not overcome it."

JOHN 16:33
"I have told you these things, so that in Me you may have peace. In this world you will have trouble. But take heart! I have overcome the world." (NIV)

In our passage for today, Paul and Timothy reminded the Colossians that they are in the kingdom of light. We all need the reminder that we are in the kingdom of light, the Light that has overcome the darkness! Because of Jesus' death and resurrection, we know something other than the dark that creeps in all around us in this world.

Yesterday, we held this reminder in our hands:

YOU ARE QUALIFIED. YOU ARE ENOUGH.

Today we're going to embrace this reminder:

WE LIVE IN THE LIGHT.

What kinds of things first come to mind when you think about "living in the light"?

According to Colossians 1:12–14, how did we get from darkness to light?

We don't magically get from point A to point B, dark to light. We need a mediator, a redeemer, and God made a way through His Son. Jesus came down to earth and gave His life so that we might have life. His resurrection defeated death and sin's grip once and for all. In our Baptism, we die with Christ. He drowns the power of sin and death in our lives, and then we rise with Him to share in the new life He brings, which will never end. Christ did something no one else could ever do. He defeated all darkness for forever.

In the passage, circle each action that God took for our benefit:

... giving thanks to the Father, who has qualified you to share in the inheritance of the saints in light. He has delivered us from the domain of darkness and transferred us to the kingdom of His beloved Son, in whom we have redemption, the forgiveness of sins. (Colossians 1:12–14)

We can map the passage like this:

QUALIFIED ▸ DELIVERED ▸ TRANSFERRED ▸ REDEEMED ▸ FORGIVEN

I cheated a little bit. The last two words in the map are different from the words in Colossians 1:14. *Redemption* and *forgiveness* aren't verbs, are they? (I promise I passed English class!) But forgiveness and redemption do stem from verbs. And God took these actions for our benefit, just as He took the other actions mentioned in these verses—the sacrifices a mighty God made to save His family members. And He continues to take these actions for us, over and over again, throughout our lives. Let's look at each of God's actions.

WE ARE **QUALIFIED.**

By Christ's death and resurrection, you are enough. You are enough because the price has been paid for your sin. I know the world really, really wants us to think there is something more, something else we need. But we're going to believe God:

FORGIVEN = ENOUGH

The passage map starts and ends with forgiveness.

What are some of the world's messages about qualification? How are these very different from the message of forgiveness and grace in Jesus alone?

WE ARE **DELIVERED** AND **TRANSFERRED.**

RESCUE AND DELIVERANCE IN THE OLD TESTAMENT
God has always been the rescuer of His people, pointing them to the rescue to come for all people in Jesus Christ, through His acts of deliverance in the Old Testament. See examples of Israel proclaiming God's deliverance in Psalm 22:4–5 and 77:13–15.

After mankind sinned, we lived in darkness, separated from God. Isolation from our fellow human beings feels lonely. But isolation from God has spiritual weight, the weight of darkness. And that weight eventually leads to death. Christ came to snatch us from the devil's grasp. He told the evil one, "Stand down!" Jesus rescued us from Satan's domain by dying and rising for us. Jesus made it possible for us to have a relationship with Him again and transferred us to His kingdom of light. Mightily and mysteriously, who He is and what He has done become true of us, as a gift.

We still see the darkness for now. But on a day that is coming soon, we will see the fulfillment of Jesus' victory over darkness. Though there is still darkness around me, Christ has delivered me and continuously delivers me from the crippling weight of that darkness.

I am still a sinner. My default is and is going to continue to be sin. Yet I'm new in Jesus. It's a mystery. It's complicated. And Satan uses all of this complication to his benefit, trying to convince us to sit in shame when we sin or to try to hide our sins away, avoiding relationship with God and those who could help us.

What are some ways that people try to hide their sins in adulthood?

Shame is Satan's attempt to convince us we are unforgivable. Christ's death begs to differ. When Christ died on the cross, our consequences became His. The punishment of our sin was transferred onto Him. There are times we can't see Jesus with us. Sometimes we don't *feel* forgiven. We struggle to see

Him working through us and in us. But Christ works His light in our lives every day anyway. He sees me in my hurt and my brokenness and brings light into my life with His hope, every day.

WE ARE REDEEMED AND LIVING IN FORGIVENESS.

Redemption means we do not live in the darkness, nor do we *belong* to the darkness.

THERE IS SOMETHING TRANSFORMING ABOUT KNOWING DARKNESS DOESN'T REIGN.

Write out 1 Thessalonians 5:5 as a reminder of our identity in the light that reigns:

Redemption intersects with our everyday surrounded-by-darkness struggles—those school shootings, divorce, all that gossip, loss—in their many and various forms.

What surrounded-by-darkness struggles would you add to the list?

Christ's redemption comes in and can make anything new, restored, transformed, transferred. He can take our darkest heartache and our deepest shame and make it beautiful in His time.

Paul knew the feeling of being surrounded by darkness in very real ways. What physical darkness did Paul experience according to Acts 9:9?

Paul, the one who had persecuted so many Christians, was transformed and fully restored. See Acts 9:17–18. How did Paul experience this both physically and spiritually?

Yet what kinds of darkness did Paul experience (described in Acts 9:22–25) even after Jesus miraculously redeemed, transformed, and restored him?

We so badly want darkness to disappear entirely; unfortunately, this side of heaven, it doesn't work that way. Even when we surround ourselves with good things, noble things, honorable things, darkness is going to fight to entrap people until Christ comes again. And yet we live in confidence that we have been redeemed from the darkness. It has no hold on us anymore because we are forgiven people who also forgive others.

Brainstorm some ways we can live in the light of truth, reflecting Jesus, even when the world we physically stand in is so dark.

THE CHURCH: LAMPSTAND AND LIGHT-BEARERS

Our job as the Church in the midst of a dark world is not only to rest in the truth that the darkness no longer has a hold on us. Our job is also to be light-bearers, bringing Jesus, the true light, to the world. People outside the Church are looking every which way, trying to find what makes sense of life. Though they are seeking light, they will never be able to see anything but darkness on their own. The struggle of knowing something is missing but being unable to figure it out shows itself sometimes as feelings of despair or being overwhelmed about life, or as anger, frustration, hurtfulness, condescension, contempt, and persecution toward Christians. But instead of being afraid of how people outside the Church might respond, our job is to show them Jesus, the true light, as clearly as we can. The only thing that is truly of the light is whatever points people to Jesus.

As Simeon said when he saw baby Jesus in the temple long ago:

" . . . because of the tender mercy of our God,

whereby the sunrise shall visit us from on high

to give light to those who sit in darkness and in the shadow of death,

to guide our feet into the way of peace."

(Luke 1:78–79)

The forgiveness of God, the tender mercy of Jesus, brings the sunrise into our lives and gives light amidst the darkness all around.

Jesus, the true light, shines and shines hard through His Church into all the dark places. The darkness still presses in, but we see Christ, we hear Christ, we teach Christ, and we exist in the light of Christ, even in the midst of the dark, until He comes again and there is only light.

Connected by the Word

Use the Scripture memory verse for the week and the prayer prompt to bring your confession, thanksgiving, praise, and requests before our mighty and mysterious God.

Week 1 Memory Verse

Since we heard of your faith in Christ Jesus and of the love that you have for all the saints. (Colossians 1:4)

Prayer Prompt

Lord of light, You bring forgiveness and mercy where there is only hurt and hatred. Help us to shine Your light into our homes and the world around us . . .

"In Christ" Scavenger Hunt

"In Christ" is one of the most common phrases found throughout all the New Testament letters, and many of these references are found in Paul's letters. The word *in* may seem to be a small detail, but it speaks mercy. *In* means we have a relationship with God in Christ, and that relationship brings us salvation. "In Christ" means yesterday, today, and forever He is at work in me. "In Christ" invites me into constant conversation with God as a member of His family.

Use this list of Scripture verses to find many of the references to "in Christ" in Paul's writing, according to the ESV translation. What promise does being "in Christ" hold for you in each verse?

Romans 3:22–24		2 Corinthians 1:21–22	
Romans 6:3–4		2 Corinthians 2:14–17	
Romans 6:11		2 Corinthians 5:17–19	
Romans 8:1–2		2 Corinthians 12:19	
Romans 8:38–39		Galatians 2:4	
Romans 9:1		Galatians 2:16–17	
1 Corinthians 1:2–4		Galatians 3:14	
1 Corinthians 1:30		Galatians 3:26–28	
1 Corinthians 3:1		Galatians 5:6	
1 Corinthians 4:10–17		Ephesians 1:1–3	
1 Corinthians 15:18–19		Ephesians 1:9–12	
2 Corinthians 1:5		Ephesians 2:6–7	

Ephesians 2:10–13		Colossians 2:5–6	
Ephesians 3:6		1 Thessalonians 1:3	
Ephesians 3:20–21		1 Thessalonians 4:16	
Ephesians 4:32		1 Thessalonians 5:18	
Philippians 1:1		2 Thessalonians 1:1	
Philippians 1:26–27		1 Timothy 1:14–16	
Philippians 2:1–2		2 Timothy 1:1	
Philippians 2:4–5		2 Timothy 1:9	
Philippians 3:9		2 Timothy 1:13	
Philippians 3:14		2 Timothy 2:1–3	
Philippians 4:7		2 Timothy 2:10–13	
Philippians 4:19–21		Philemon 8–9	
Colossians 1:2–4		Philemon 20	
Colossians 1:24		Philemon 23	
Colossians 1:28			

Week 2

ALL THAT IS MADE

Viewer Guide

VIDEO 2: ON MYSTERY AND REVEALING
COLOSSIANS 1:15–2:3

VERSES TO BOOKMARK
Colossians 1:24–29

2 CORINTHIANS 12:9
"My grace is sufficient for you, for My power is made perfect in weakness."

God does not _____ things from us.

SEE COLOSSIANS 1:24–29.

THE MYSTERY

THE MYSTERY OF GOD
When we talk about mystery in relation to the Word of God and the person of God, we are not talking about Sherlock Holmes–style mysteries about unknown events. In the cultural framework of the New Testament, "mystery" was always connected to what is sacred. The Greek word *mystērion* (μυστήριον) was always used in relation to spiritual ideas and discussions in ancient Greek writings and in the New Testament.*

1. The mystery is _____ by God.

SEE COLOSSIANS 1:24–25.

2. The mystery *was* _____ but is now _____.

SEE COLOSSIANS 1:26.

ISAIAH 55:8–9
"For My thoughts are not your thoughts, neither are your ways My ways, declares the LORD. For as the heavens are higher than the earth, so are My ways higher than your ways and My thoughts than your thoughts."

3. The mystery comes to the world through God's _____ and God's

_____.

SEE COLOSSIANS 1:27.

4. The mystery is _____ about Jesus and is always _____.

οἰκονομία
oikonomia: administration, stewardship, management of household affairs.**

* W. Bauer, F. W. Danker, W. F. Arndt, and F. W. Gingrich, "μυστήριον, ου, τό," *Greek-English Lexicon of the New Testament and Other Early Christian Literature*, 3rd ed. (Chicago, IL: University of Chicago Press, 1999), 661–62.
*** Bible Hub, s.v. "3622. oikonomia," https://biblehub.com/greek/3622.htm.

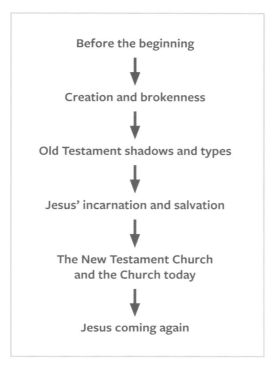

Before the beginning

↓

Creation and brokenness

↓

Old Testament shadows and types

↓

Jesus' incarnation and salvation

↓

The New Testament Church
and the Church today

↓

Jesus coming again

EPHESIANS 1:13–14
"And you also were included in Christ when you heard the message of truth, the gospel of your salvation. When you believed, you were marked in Him with a seal, the promised Holy Spirit, who is a deposit guaranteeing our inheritance until the redemption of those who are God's possession—to the praise of His glory." (NIV)

ESCHATOLOGY
The study of the end times; particularly, the study of how God will resolve the brokenness of the world and will usher in the new creation when Jesus returns.

DISCUSSION QUESTIONS

1. In the following Bible verses, what can we learn about the mystery of God? How do the insights about mystery in these verses fit with what we learned about mystery in today's video segment?

   Romans 16:25–27

   1 Corinthians 15:50–53

   Ephesians 1:5–10

   Ephesians 3:1–6

2. What confounds you regarding who God is and what He has done? What characteristics or actions of God are hard for you to wrap your head around?

3. Tell us about a time a Bible verse powerfully stood out to you in a surprising way, like my experience with Susan and 2 Corinthians 12:9 in college.

Day 1

CREATOR OF ALL
COLOSSIANS 1:15–17

My husband and daughter recently went on a trip to Malawi, Africa, to work with our ministry partners there. During some downtime, they were able to go on a safari to enjoy the beauty of a continent so different from our own.

Not to be outdone, I took the other three children to the zoo.

You cannot walk around a zoo without experiencing at least one moment of wonder. During this particular zoo visit, we saw zebras, each with a different stripe pattern than the next; giraffes ambling, neck first, carrying around dignity like they own the place; playful penguins trying to make new friends and steal the show; a sea turtle so statuesque, we were unsure if he was real, pressed against the glass tunnel.

Everyone should go to the zoo once in a while. We all need a moment to step into intentional wonder.

Today the Book of Colossians teaches us the value of wonder as well as careful, thoughtful investigation. Each has a different purpose, but both impact our relationship with God—Father, Son, and Spirit—the mighty and the mysterious Creator of all.

When we lose wonder or we forget to slow down enough to wonder, we can also easily forget about God as Creator, an important part of God's identity. So for today's lesson, I want this to be our refrain:

GOD IS CREATOR AS MUCH AS HE IS SAVIOR, REDEEMER, AND RESTORER.

Let's begin at the beginning, or really, before the beginning. Read Genesis 1:1. Write it in the space below to help it stick in your brain. Why is this short verse profound?

Before the first moment of creation, there was no time, no need for time, no beginning, no end, no ground to walk on, no sea to sail, no sun to rise or set. Before anything existed, before we existed, God existed. Before *anything*, He was—and He is, and He is to come.

Like Genesis 1–2, the Book of Colossians also helps us reflect on the gravity, breadth, and depth of God's creation alongside its beauty.

Turn to Colossians 1:15–17. How do the words in those verses connect to Genesis 1:1–3?

AUTHOR'S NOTE
The density of the language and imagery Paul uses in Colossians 1:15–20 leads many commentators to suggest that these verses are actually a hymn or song. Paul may have written these lines to be a song of praise to the Creator, Redeemer, and Sustainer of the universe, or he may have taken a song the Colossians already knew that was written by someone else and was circulating in the Early Church. There is speculation about the kind of false teaching that this hymn is addressing, perhaps a false teaching gaining popularity in Colossae or elsewhere in the Early Church. Regardless of the origin of these verses, they give deep descriptions of Christ that believers meditated on then, that we can meditate on now, and that Christians will continue to meditate on until Jesus comes back again.

Before opening this study, did you know that Colossians is about creation? I certainly didn't. Actually, full disclosure here: I set out to write a Bible study on Genesis 1 and 2, but as I tried to understand God's creation, I came across the short Letter to the Colossians. Eventually this letter took over and became the topic of the Bible study! Sometimes God turns us to the obvious. Other times, He turns us to a fuller picture than what we realized was there.

Can you see Colossians pointing us back to Genesis, and Genesis pointing us forward to Colossians? God's Word is connected in ways we can spend a lifetime discovering. God intends us to read His Word as a collection of separate writings, but also as a unified whole. When we don't understand something in one passage, He gives us the gift of being able to read other passages in His Word that address related topics in order to help us understand.

In Genesis, we find God creating. In Colossians, we learn that our Savior, Jesus, participated in that creating. Colossians enables us to see God's act of creating in a clearer light.

Colossians has a lot to say, and a lot we will tackle together. But we will see that the foundation of Colossians is this:

JESUS IS ALL. FROM CREATION TO NEW CREATION, HE IS ALL.

GOD IS CREATOR AS MUCH AS HE IS SAVIOR, REDEEMER, AND RESTORER.

Over the next few days, we will focus on Colossians 1:15–19, and we will reflect on the image of God, the care of God, and the authority of God. For today's study though, pay close attention to the creative and sustaining nature of God, and how His intimate care permeates His actions. As you read Colossians 1:15–17 again, circle or take note of anything related to *Jesus* as Creator:

> He is the image of the invisible God, the firstborn of all creation. For by Him all things were created, in heaven and on earth, visible and invisible, whether thrones or dominions or rulers or authorities—all things were created through Him and for Him. And He is before all things, and in Him all things hold together.
> (Colossians 1:15–17)

Colossians 1:15–19 is full of complex statements. But these verses actually give us a framework for our whole study: Jump into the mysterious, while also being surrounded by the comfort and clarity of Jesus as all.

Every single thing on this planet, every single thing in the heavens above, every single thing invisible or visible was created by Jesus and created for Jesus. Created *by Him* and created *for Him* are such important ideas, so let's look at them individually as we reflect on creation.

By Jesus

JOHN 1:1–3
"In the beginning was the Word, and the Word was with God, and the Word was God. He was in the beginning with God. All things were made through Him, and without Him was not any thing made that was made."

We believe in God the Father, God the Son, and God the Holy Spirit—three persons, one God. "Three in one" means each person of the Godhead was there before the beginning, is there now transcending the world we see, and will be there throughout eternity. All things were created through God the Son, Jesus. And then He also became part of His creation by becoming man. He carried out God's plan of salvation in creation: He died a true, human death on a cross made from trees and rose again to new life after being placed in a rock-cut tomb.

Jesus' relationship with creation as both God and man is a mystery we cannot fully understand. There is a tension that exists: Jesus is fully man, but He is also fully God—uncreated and eternally existing. Colossians 1:15–17 affirms both, without explaining how they can both be true:

- Jesus is "before all things" (1:17)—He is not created; He existed eternally, before creation.

- And yet Jesus is "the firstborn of all creation" (1:15)—He became man to be our Savior.

We see this mystery reflected in the way Jesus interacted with His creation during His time on earth.

Look through each of the following Gospel accounts. How do the events in each passage reflect Jesus' unique relationship with His creation—being fully God and fully man?

Matthew 14:22–33

Mark 8:1–13

Luke 22:39–44

John 21:1–14

Jesus was born of a woman. Being born and having a mother are part of creation. Jesus was born in a particular place called Bethlehem, under the jurisdiction of a certain government. And He counted thirty-three birthdays from then on. All these things are part of creation. Jesus physically healed men and women from diseases and defects by means of mud, water, or words spoken with His vocal cords—all part of creation. Jesus held people's hands, shed tears, and ate His veggies—all part of creation. How meaningful is it to realize that Jesus made creation . . . entered creation . . . sustains creation . . . renews creation . . . holds creation in His hands . . . and loves creation, including you and me.

Jesus clearly is not a distant God. This creation is His—even more than our houses or our families are ours. We care for our house and our family. We interact with them daily, check in with them, love on them, and boast in them. How much more so, then, does Jesus do this for the creation that belongs to Him?! And we do these things selfishly and imperfectly, but Jesus does all of this for His creation in perfect love and perfect authority. He continues to create every day.

Think about the world around you, right where you are. Where do you see Jesus caring, sustaining, and interacting today?

What is the significance of realizing everything was made *by* Jesus?

In Colossians, Paul reminds us specifically that all that is "visible and invisible, whether thrones or dominions or rulers or authorities" (1:16) is created by Jesus. How does this truth also shape our perspective?

FOR JESUS

But creation is not only made *by* Jesus. It is also made *for* Jesus.

Small words can easily be missed. Colossians 1:16 makes a big use of small words—specifically, the little words *all* and *for*.

What even is *all*? What are some things that come to mind for you under the umbrella of *all* in Colossians 1:16?

ACTIVITY
Sometimes it's fun and useful to remind ourselves how creative and awesome God is. Here's a small activity to help you think about God's creativity, as you reflect on Colossians 1:16:

Name 15 people created by God.

Name 15 animals created by God.

Name 15 foods created by God.

Name 15 places created by God.

All things were created *for* Jesus. Every little thing. Every big thing. Every supernova, every beating heart, every dolphin song, every playful penguin, every breath, every breeze, every zoo, every African safari is for Him.

We can walk around pretending it's all for us. We can walk around pretending it all exists to serve the good of humankind. But Colossians 1:16 makes plain the truth of who all this is for.

ALL THAT EXISTS IS FOR JESUS.

Everything my eyes behold has been made to bring Him glory. He is the one who fills my lungs with every breath I take. When I buy bananas at the grocery store, they were His idea: He grew them through sunshine, rain, and the hands of a farmer thousands of miles away from my home in Nebraska.

But then, just when I think I'm starting to get the hang of what it means for *all* things to be created *for* Him, it gets harder and more complicated. When the earth quakes, does that bring Him glory? When winds roar, how is that for Jesus? These are questions we won't have complete answers to until He comes back again. While the idea of God's creation involving loss and aggression is difficult and beyond what I can understand, I'd rather stand in the truth that all things are for Him than be left to endure this shaking world unaware and wondering literally who in the world is in charge. Because it's all for Him, I can rest in Him, run to Him, cling to Him, and find hope in Him—even in the middle of the challenges and the things that come into my life and don't seem good to me at first glance . . . or at any glance.

All things created *by* and *for* Jesus means our mighty and mysterious Savior is also our mighty and mysterious Creator:

GOD IS CREATOR AS MUCH AS HE IS SAVIOR, REDEEMER, AND RESTORER.

JESUS IS ALL. FROM CREATION TO NEW CREATION, HE IS ALL.

CONNECTED BY THE WORD

Use the Scripture memory verse for the week and the prayer prompt to bring your confession, thanksgiving, praise, and requests before our mighty and mysterious God.

WEEK 2 MEMORY VERSE

And He is before all things, and in Him all things hold together. (Colossians 1:17)

PRAYER PROMPT

Dear Creator, You make all and You offer salvation to all people. Lord, help us to see You creating and sustaining all things around us, including . . .

GOD AND SCIENCE

God can use science to do the miraculous, and God can do the miraculous without science. God set the boundary lines of nature that we find in biology, chemistry, physics, and other areas of scientific study. But God isn't bound by those boundary lines Himself.

Science and Jesus fit together—like oceans and beaches, the savanna and acacia trees, the forest and lichen—because He was there when each tiny element of science was created. He is the Creator of all.

When confronted with uncomfortable arguments about evolution or big environmental topics like global warming, it can be tempting to gravitate toward buffet-style Christianity: "I'll take the Jesus who loves everybody, but when I get to the Jesus who claims to have created all things, that looks a little too salty, so I'll pass on that." But Jesus is either *all* (as the Bible tells us He is), or He isn't *all*.

It's helpful to remember that God and science aren't at odds; they are in harmony. As believers in Christ, we start with God's Word first and let it shape our understanding of the world, as we are then informed by research and science. We don't start with research and science and decide whether God's Word fits or doesn't fit into our worldview.

So Will I (100 Billion X)

God of creation
There at the start
Before the beginning of time
With no point of reference
You spoke to the dark
And fleshed out the wonder of light

And as You speak
A hundred billion galaxies are born
In the vapor of Your breath the planets form
If the stars were made to worship so will I
I can see Your heart in everything You've made
Every burning star
A signal fire of grace
If creation sings Your praises so will I

God of Your promise
You don't speak in vain
No syllable empty or void
For once You have spoken
All nature and science
Follow the sound of Your voice

And as You speak
A hundred billion creatures catch Your breath
Evolving in pursuit of what You said
If it all reveals Your nature so will I
I can see Your heart in everything You say
Every painted sky
A canvas of Your grace
If creation still obeys You so will I
So will I
So will I

If the stars were made to worship so will I
If the mountains bow in reverence so will I
If the oceans roar Your greatness so will I
For if everything exists to lift You high so will I
If the wind goes where You send it so will I

If the rocks cry out in silence so will I
If the sum of all our praises still falls shy
Then we'll sing again a hundred billion times

God of salvation
You chased down my heart
Through all of my failure and pride
On a hill You created
The light of the world
Abandoned in darkness to die

And as You speak
A hundred billion failures disappear
Where You lost Your life so I could find it here
If You left the grave behind You so will I
I can see Your heart in everything You've done
Every part designed in a work of art called love
If You gladly chose surrender so will I
I can see Your heart
Eight billion different ways
Every precious one
A child You died to save
If You gave Your life to love them so will I

Like You would again a hundred billion times
But what measure could amount to Your desire
You're the One who never leaves the one behind

—Hillsong United
Written by Joel Houston, Benjamin Hastings, and Michael Fatkin

Day 2

IMAGE OF ALL
COLOSSIANS 1:15–17

In our small congregation in northwest Ohio, we took Vacation Bible School (VBS) very seriously. It's amazing how much life a five-day celebration of Jesus can bring to a church and community.

Our senior high youth and college students were usually helpers during the VBS craziness. Their role at VBS was often very practical: saving preschoolers from running into the parking lot, fetching more snack when someone's snack spilled, and giving out hugs. The other part of their role was sheer energy. They had an unspoken duty to raise the morale of the whole operation. People using their hands and feet to serve in the life of a congregation speaks love because serving says, "I'm invested." When young adults or anyone in a congregation lets their excitement out, grace becomes tangible because their attitude loudly proclaims, "I want to be here for Jesus and for you."

The world is hard. Sadness is real. Churches face struggles and challenges all the time. Once a year, we need a little VBS joy in our midst. VBS does take infinite amounts of work, but it brings so much joy because it's one example in the life of the church when we get to see something tangible from the faith we normally celebrate as invisible.

Hebrews 11:1–3 reminds us:

> Now faith is the assurance of things hoped for, the conviction of things not seen. For by it the people of old received their commendation. By faith we understand that the universe was created by the word of God, so that what is seen was not made out of things that are visible.

(Hebrews 11:1–3)

Colossians 1:15–17 also rests on the invisible:

> He is the image of the invisible God, the

firstborn of all creation. For by Him all things were created, in heaven and on earth, visible and invisible, whether thrones or dominions or rulers or authorities—all things were created through Him and for Him. And He is before all things, and in Him all things hold together.

(Colossians 1:15–17)

If God were never visible to us, He would still be God. However, God in His mercy does make Himself visible to us. He made Himself visible to us once and for all time when Jesus took on our flesh and came among us two thousand years ago. And He still mercifully makes Himself visible to us today. He does this through His Word, through Baptism and Holy Communion, through the forgiveness of our sins spoken aloud from our pastor or a friend, and—as we said about VBS a few paragraphs earlier—through fellow Christians. In today's study, we'll talk about some of these ways we see our mighty and mysterious God.

As we learned yesterday, many commentators think Colossians 1:15–20 is a song or hymn that Paul wanted to include with his letter of teaching and exhortation to the Colossians. Read this song as a whole segment now, rather than in broken-up parts as we have done so far. What does this song tell you about Jesus, the one who reveals God to us?

Jesus is the image of the invisible God. God—in His fullness—is so glorious, He is unseeable. *Unseeable* is not a word. I made it up to mean "something we can't see with our physical eyes because it is so beyond our understanding."

For example, in the Old Testament, Moses wanted to see God tangibly and gaze on His face. Moses already had a close relationship with God. But he wanted to know God even more by seeing God with his eyes. Yet God loved Moses enough to shield him from fully seeing His mightiness, His glory, because seeing it would actually kill Moses. Just as God knows better than us, God knew better than Moses too.

Turn to Exodus 33:13–23. What was the outcome of Moses' attempt to gaze on the face of an unseeable God?

Even though God in His full glory is unseeable, yet He made man and woman to be in His image, unique in His creation. God intended that every time we gaze at another human being, we would glimpse a small shadow of our great God's existence. Every ethnicity, every shape or size, every race, every age of mankind is an imprint of the Maker of the universe. Coins are imprinted with leaders' faces; copies are imprinted from famous works of art.[8] These imprints look strikingly similar to the original, but they can also be distinguished from the original in important ways. Likewise, we are imprints of our Creator.

When I was a little girl, I remember standing beside my mom in church. She let me wear her cardigan during the sermon or play with her big beaded necklace. My mom nurtured and cared for me in these small ways, as well as big ones. While she is imperfect, and God is absolutely perfect, this is one way I came to understand who God is, His imprint as nurturer and caregiver of His people.

Who has shown you God's imprint as Creator and Caretaker in your life?

In AD 0 (give or take a few years), God brought His one and only true image to be among us on the earth. This was not an imprint. This was God Himself. This is what Paul means when he says that Jesus is "the image of the invisible God."

However, trying to understand and verbalize what it means for the invisible God to make Himself visible in a human being is a struggle. We are not alone in that struggle.

Christians in the fourth century AD—roughly three hundred years after Paul's Letter to the Colossians—came together and did the best they could to put into words what it means for Jesus to be "the image of the invisible God."[9] The result was what we call the Nicene Creed. This creed has united believers ever since in a common confession of Jesus' two natures: fully God and fully man.[10]

One section of the Nicene Creed recounts and proclaims Jesus Christ as Lord in unique and beautifully repetitive language. It strikes me that this is similar to the words of the song in Colossians 1:15–20. Both reassure us that Jesus is the very image of God. The Nicene Creed says:

AND IN ONE LORD JESUS CHRIST, THE ONLY-BEGOTTEN SON OF GOD, BEGOTTEN OF HIS FATHER BEFORE ALL WORLDS, GOD OF GOD, LIGHT OF LIGHT, VERY GOD OF VERY GOD.

One of the prominent false teachings in Colossae before Paul sent his letter was that Jesus could be either God or man, but not both. Even though Paul and the other apostles in the New Testament addressed these issues, such false teachings did not die out. Eventually, Christians formed the Nicene Creed as a definitive response.

There will always be false teachers and confusion about who this Jesus truly is. Tools developed years ago by Christians, tools like the Nicene Creed and Paul's Spirit-inspired song in Colossians 1:15–20, help us to more clearly define our faith, proclaim our faith, and share our faith.

The false teachers in Colossae found Jesus as the image of the invisible God hard to believe. And we can empathize that this truth is not easy to understand. Yet the way we approach things that are hard to understand is that we continue to read God's Word, especially passages on topics related to what we are struggling with, and we talk about God's Word with others. Ultimately, we believe what God says and take Him at His Word because He is the one who says it. We trust Him because He is the God who is our Savior and Creator. And sometimes we just let His mystery remain, well, a mystery.

According to Hebrews 11:1–3, what do we lean on when we struggle to take God at His Word?

Things may look fuzzy now and may remain fuzzier far longer than we would like.

> For now we see in a mirror dimly, but then face to face. Now I know in part; then I shall know fully, even as I have been fully known.
> (1 Corinthians 13:12)

We see Jesus only in part right now, like a video-chat or old-family-movie version of someone we love. As pilgrims on this journey, that sustains us; but it doesn't satisfy us. We want to be closer to Him. Rest assured: although we see only in part now, one day very soon we will see in full. Then it will be worth the wait.

And as we wait, we meet with Him where He has promised to be. God never leaves us without ways to draw close to Him. When we read God's Word, Jesus—the God of God, Light of light, very God of very God—illuminates our souls through His Spirit. In my local church, we say the Nicene Creed before we take Communion. This is not an accident. We confess our faith in Jesus through the Creed. Then we sit at our Savior's table, where Jesus feeds us His body and blood under the bread and wine. In Communion, we receive His grace both visibly and invisibly until we get to see Him face-to-face.

AUTHOR'S NOTE
The Book of John is another great place to find assurance of Jesus as both fully God and fully man. What do the following verses have to say about our Savior's nature as both God and man?

John 1:14

John 1:18

John 14:9

71

HE IS THE IMAGE OF GOD, FIRSTBORN OF ALL.

HE IS THE MIGHTY AND THE MYSTERIOUS.

CONNECTED BY THE WORD

Use the Scripture memory verse for the week and the prayer prompt to bring your confession, thanksgiving, praise, and requests before our mighty and mysterious God.

WEEK 2 MEMORY VERSE

And He is before all things, and in Him all things hold together. (Colossians 1:17)

PRAYER PROMPT

Jesus, You are the image of the invisible God. There are things about You I don't understand at times. I lay these things before You today . . .

Day 3

I am an avid podcast subscriber. Podcasts give you short bursts of information with lots of nuggets of knowledge, usually in the shape of fun banter or heartfelt monologues. I also love reading and pick up lots of articles from the interwebs. I like TV, but I rarely check television news report because seeing the evil in the world depicted visually pushes all my anxiety buttons.

What platforms are your favorite for (literally or figuratively) downloading information and ideas? How do you like to learn information and new knowledge?

I was listening to a podcast recently in which the host used the word *meta* more than once in the episode. This was a new word for me, one of those words that sounds familiar but whose definition eludes you. After thirty minutes of listening to the podcast and trying to remember my third-grade lessons on context clues, I still couldn't place what the host meant by *meta*. So, I did what any self-respecting vocabulary-loving girl would do: I looked it up on the internet.

What did I find? I found myself knee-deep in a current stream of arguments about what *meta* actually is. Unfortunately, the internet doesn't always have quick and easy answers either. After lots of investigating, I came to this conclusion: *Meta* is frequently used as an adjective describing something that is self-referential, someone or something talking about itself. However, *meta* is also being used in a way that is more complicated than simply self-reference. The definition that seems to still be developing is *meta* as analyzing something on an abstract level that can quickly cause brain freeze—without the joy of a slushie.

I'm going to take a stab at using this newly acquired word:

COLOSSIANS IS VERY META.

Colossians is the Body of Christ—Paul, Timothy, and the recipients of the letter—exploring and considering (with the Holy Spirit's guiding) what it means to be the Body of Christ. Similarly, Colossians is people who have the Spirit of the living God in their bodies exploring and considering the nature of this living God.

Whoa. We might as well get our slushies now, so we can fully enjoy the brain freeze.

Read through Colossians 1:15–20 and let the mind-bending-ness of it wash over you. Rejoice in it a little.

Where else do you see the spirit of exploration and contemplation in Colossians 1?

The problem with the meta about God is that we'll inevitably run into a lot we can't understand. Since God invites us into an intimate relationship with Him through Christ, we expect that relationship to be similar to our most comfortable, understandable, and relatable relationships with people. But God, while relatable and while intimate with us, will always be bigger than us. Even though it can be uncomfortable to acknowledge that He is a great big mighty and mysterious God whom we do not fully understand, this is part of what it means for Him to be the Creator and us to be the creatures. We did not create Him, so we do not fully understand Him. However, He created us and fully understands us.

When our limited understanding of God's mightiness in Scripture concerns us, we hold onto what we do understand: Jesus died on the cross and rose again from the dead for us. This is why it is so important that Jesus is the image of the invisible God, as we talked about yesterday. All that we need to know for salvation is clear through Jesus. And even in Colossians 1:17–19, in the midst of the meta, this reality about our crucified, risen, and ascended Savior is very clear: Jesus is in charge. He is in charge in our realm here on earth and in heaven above.

JESUS IS OVER ALL.

Read Colossians 1:17–19 on the opposite page, and circle or note the words or phrases that could be used as titles for Jesus, in light of who He is and what He does.

And He is before all things, and in Him all things hold together. And He is the head of the body, the church. He is the beginning, the firstborn from the dead, that in everything He might be preeminent. For in Him all the fullness of God was pleased to dwell. (Colossians 1:17–19)

The word *preeminent* sums up this small section. Jesus' place in the entirety of the universe is first, foremost, greatest, most important, chief. Jesus as preeminent means He is *over all* in the simplest sense—He is in charge. It also means many other things.

Let's dive into some of the specifics of what Paul says about Christ as preeminent, such as Christ before all and Christ holding all things together. Some of this is meta. If you start to feel the brain freeze at some point, don't despair. This same Jesus took on human flesh to die for you and rise again from the dead. All of this meta about Jesus doesn't change that. It only adds to our understanding of the significance of what Jesus has done.

Before All

Colossians 1:17 reminds us Jesus is before all things. The phrase "before all things" holds a double meaning. Jesus existed before our timeline, before day one of creation. And He is before all things in authority because God the Father gave Jesus authority over all things. Jesus' authority over all things was sometimes visible during His earthly ministry. Sometimes people were very grateful for His authority. Other times they asked, "Who does this guy think He is?"

Look up the following passages. How do people receive glimpses of Jesus' preeminence in these passages? How do they respond? How does Jesus exemplify preeminence, while still remaining very much the humble servant we might be more comfortable seeing as our Savior?

Mark 1:21–28

John 2:13–22

PREEMINENCE
That which is supreme, having inarguable leadership, authority, and superiority; that which completely surpasses all other things. Jesus' preeminence means that He is Lord and Master of the universe and of our hearts and lives.

AUTHOR'S NOTE
The Greek word translated as "preeminence" is used nowhere else in Scripture.[19] However, the concept of Christ's preeminence is present in many parts of the Bible, such as John 3:31 and Hebrews 1:3–4.

πρωτεύω
prōteuō: to be in first place, chief, preeminent.

Our sinful human nature wants to balk at God's authority. We like His authority when it serves us and does what we think is good. But when God does or says something in His authority that we don't like, we push against it and think a better solution would be simply changing God's rules to fit our own.

Where in life do you struggle with Christ's authority, or when have you ever wanted Him to exert a more obvious authority?

It never goes well when we try to change God's rules to fit into ours. That's what the people tried to do when they crucified Jesus instead of believing He was God's true Messiah. God's Word testifies that when Jesus returns, those who have rejected His authority will receive the fruition of choosing their own authority instead of Jesus'. Whether we like it or not, Jesus has authority over all things, as Colossians 1:18 describes:

And He is the head of the body, the church. He is the beginning, the _____ _____ _____ _____ , that in everything He might be preeminent.

Christ was over everything, over all. However, He was willing to be humiliated not only by taking on human flesh but also by dying on a cross. In His glorious resurrection, Christ shows us He is not only Lord of Life, but Lord over death as well.

BEFORE ALL HIS PEOPLE

Colossians 1:18 also reminds us Christ is before His people and before any individual among His people. He existed before the Church, He is in charge of the Church, and He holds the Church together. It seems obvious: if Christ is in charge of the whole world as Creator and Savior, then of course He's in charge of the Church! But for something as messy and complicated as our life together in the Church, it's helpful to intentionally note this. The Church on earth and we as individuals in that Church need constant reminders of who is in charge.

Where do you see struggles to recognize Christ's authority in the church today?

Why is it hard for even the church to completely accept Christ's authority?

GOD'S AUTHORITY AND THE CHURCH

Many of the earliest followers of Jesus in the New Testament churches struggled with God's authority when they began to understand that He wants every race, tribe, nation, and people to be part of the Body of Christ. We may or may not struggle with similar prejudice in our churches, but many of us do often think God should treat people differently, depending on how "bad" their sins are. For more on this age-old struggle, turn to Matthew 20:1–16 and be encouraged! Jesus is over all—for our good—when we like it and when we don't, when we understand it and when we don't.

This past summer, our college student Bible study went through the book *I Am Second*. Near the end of the book was a section called "Who Is First?" Shouldn't it be obvious to all of us within the Church who is first? It is obvious, in theory; but our sinner-saint selves will continuously struggle with authority in practice until Jesus comes again, as individuals and together as the Body of Christ. And sometimes talking about Jesus' authority in a new way can help us realize how we have been trying to hold out against His authority in some part of our life. That's what happened with our college student summer Bible study. They are all Christians, all active in worship and in the life of the congregation; most of them were baptized at a very young age. And yet the idea of God being *first* was a brand-spanking-new conceptualization for them. Honestly, it was an idea I needed to hear again as well. We as the Church fight against our natural human desire to be first every day, just as we celebrate the Savior as preeminent every day.

WE ARE SINNER-SAINTS REDEEMED AS <u>INDIVIDUALS</u> ONLY BY JESUS AND SINNER-SAINTS REDEEMED AS A <u>COMMUNITY</u> ONLY BY JESUS.

What hope does Ephesians 4:4–7 give us for the community that is the Body of Christ, even in spite of our weaknesses?

HOLDING IT ALL

One of the counterintuitive truths about Jesus' preeminence is that we, by nature, fight against it so hard, and yet it is exactly the thing we need. It is the thing that sets us free. We want to be in control of our own lives, whether our schooling, work, families, friendships, aspirations, or dreams. But the only fruit of that is anxiety as we dig ourselves in further, spinning our wheels, unable to actually control any of these things.

What things cause you the most anxiety when you try to control them?

But as I saw with our college students during our summer study, we find incredibly beautiful comfort when we embrace Christ's preeminence with everything we are—heart, soul, mind, and strength—for everything in our lives. The Holy Spirit's work to open our eyes to recognize that Jesus is first happens not once, but over and over again as we continue to grow and mature in faith.

What does Ephesians 4:11–16 say about the means God uses to help us mature in the Body of Christ?

We really do need one another. Christ can work outside of us, of course, but He has chosen to work through us to help one another grow in His Body. When we speak truth in love to one another, we share with one another the comfort that He is indeed over all things—He is in charge, not us, and He is at work in our lives. My college students often teach me even as I'm supposed to be teaching them. That's the way Jesus intended the different parts of His Body to function together, as a whole, building itself up in love, teaching and growing together. We point one another to see Christ as the head of all things.

When Colossians 1:17 says,

"In Him all things hold together,"

it means:

> Jesus is in charge of the sun and moon.
>
> Jesus is in charge of the soil and the sky.
>
> Jesus is in charge of the people in the pew and at the altar.
>
> Jesus is in charge of the cry of a newborn baby and those in the grave.

Jesus really does have the whole world in His hands, and I need the Church on earth to help me remember this promise of His is more than a children's song.

Jesus joins my heart to my lungs to pump blood and breathe fresh air. He joins my brain, my fingers, and my feet to do the work of the day. He holds all my pieces together, the broken ones too, the parts that don't quite work right in my body and my soul. He mends my past, my present, and all my tomorrows. He stitches up my wounds and heals, both wounds that are seen and those hidden deep inside. He does the same for the entire Body of Christ, piecing our lives together, healing, mending, stitching, and growing. He holds all things together.

He's got the itty-bitty baby, the wind and the rain, and you and me in His hands. In all things, Christ is preeminent—He is the mighty and the mysterious.

Now, that's meta.

CONNECTED BY THE WORD

Use the Scripture memory verse for the week and the prayer prompt to bring your confession, thanksgiving, praise, and requests before our mighty and mysterious God.

WEEK 2 MEMORY VERSE

And He is before all things, and in Him all things hold together. (Colossians 1:17)

PRAYER PROMPT

On or around the globe graphic below, write and pray for things, people, or ideas in the world, in the church, and in your life that God holds together in His hands.

Christ Jesus, You hold all things together. Your hands shape my life and all that is around me. Today I pray for . . .

Day 4

RECONCILER OF ALL
COLOSSIANS 1:19–27

Psalm 23 is probably one of the most-loved passages of Scripture, by both young and old. It doesn't seem to matter the life stage, life problem, life celebration, this psalm fits the bill every time. There are many times in life we need to know Jesus is our shepherd.

What words in Psalm 23 offer hope and meaning to you in this moment today?

Jesus, the perfect shepherd, will go out and find one lost person. He will go out and find you and me when we are lost, hurting, broken, and hard to reach. He brings us back into the sheepfold, into community with Himself and all the sheep in the herd.

MATTHEW 18:12–14
"What do you think? If a man has a hundred sheep, and one of them has gone astray, does he not leave the ninety-nine on the mountains and go in search of the one that went astray? And if he finds it, truly, I say to you, he rejoices over it more than over the ninety-nine that never went astray. So it is not the will of My Father who is in heaven that one of these little ones should perish."

In Matthew 18:12–14, we see an image of how Jesus cares for us. It's helpful to hear any day, but especially when we forget what lengths He goes to for His children. In the parable, the shepherd cares for the ninety-nine even while he goes looking for the one lost sheep. He does not abandon the ninety-nine, as if he valued the one lost sheep more than the ninety-nine. No, he leaves the ninety-nine where they will be safe and goes after the one lost sheep. All of Jesus' sheep are valuable to Him. He wants them all to be home with Him—loved and reconciled.

Today we'll sit with the reconciling work of our Savior. Open your Bibles to Colossians 1:19–22. Identify the Colossians' reality and our own reality before Jesus came to find us, as well as our reality now that we are reconciled. Use the chart below to note the words in Colossians that describe each.

Before Reconciliation	With Reconciliation

If you've ever had an estranged or strained relationship—with a parent, a sibling, a friend, or perhaps even a church—you understand the powerful emotions that are often involved. This may be a painful topic for you. However, I pray you are reminded in today's lesson that God brings hope into our lives. I pray His hope will shine on you today as you study this text.

What mental, physical, and emotional effects can be caused by estrangement or relationship stress in any person's life?

Colossians 1:21 identifies two words often associated with estrangement. Fill in these words below:

And you, who once were _____ and _____ in mind, doing evil deeds.

The word *alienated* is not just a word for someone who is a stranger. It is someone who once was close, in an intimate relationship, and now is shut out of someone else's life. Being alienated is different from never having known someone.

ἀπαλλοτριόομαι
apallotrioomai: alienated, estranged[20]

How would you describe the painful difference between being alienated (cut off from a relationship) and being a stranger (oblivious to the possibility of a relationship)?

We were estranged from God, alienated. God has always known us. He has tenderly created us, intimately loved us, known us deeply from the beginning. But our sin broke that relationship. God does not love us less. We alienated ourselves from Him in our sin, and sin's corruption made us *hostile* toward Him.

Circle or underline any words in the translations of Colossians 1:21 below that help you understand alienation from God and hostility toward Him.

NIV	NASB	NLT
Once you were alienated from God and were enemies in your minds because of your evil behavior.	And although you were formerly alienated and hostile in mind, engaged in evil deeds.	This includes you who were once far away from God. You were his enemies, separated from him by your evil thoughts and actions.

Commentator Paul E. Deterding enlightens us further about the Greek term that is translated "hostile":

In the [New Testament], . . . [this term] is used mostly, if not exclusively, to describe one who hates rather than one who is hated.[11]

The fact that Paul describes people who have not been reconciled to God through Jesus as "hostile" should give us pause as Christians. Think for a moment: What must it be like for someone to wake up every day alienated from God? What toll does it take on a person to be at odds with God every day of his or her life? Paul's powerful word *hostile* helps us realize the pain and agony of a person who lives without Jesus—whether they realize the root cause or not. If you became a Christian as a young person or an adult, you probably understand this better than those of us who can't remember not knowing Jesus. But hearing Paul briefly describe what life without Jesus is like fills us with strong compassion and genuine love for people who don't know Jesus and a compulsion to want them to be relieved of their suffering by knowing Him.

Paul can say that all people who live without Jesus are hostile toward God because hostility comes in many forms. In my experience, unbelievers most often do not believe in God because they are angry, hurt, or overwhelmed by the reality of a broken and imperfect world they can't control and don't understand—broken relationships, natural disasters, and disease, to name a few. Others are actually hostile toward God even though they seem indifferent toward Him. God's Word says that not having a relationship with God is actually having a hostile relationship with Him. If we don't believe in God according to what He has revealed about Himself through His Son—since Jesus is the image of the invisible God—we are living in opposition to God, even if we don't feel like we are opposed to Him. Not believing what God says means we despise His place as God; we would rather be our own god. That sounds harsh, but this is an important reality to recognize:

Without Jesus, there is a giant, gaping hole in our lives because

WE WERE NOT MEANT TO LIVE WITHOUT GOD.

Sometimes people are oblivious to the hole because, on their own, without God's Word or guidance, they don't know the way things should be. At other times, they feel the hole—but they don't know what is supposed to fill it. One of the clearest and most painful ways people feel the hole is when they experience other people's broken and sinful actions: abuse, assault, iniquity, shame. Sin in the world that is forced upon us, whether as children or as adults, makes us feel separated from God and alienated from Him—even when that sin isn't directly our own. It's complicated, but something being complicated doesn't mean it's any less true.

PSALM 59:2
"Deliver me from the workers of iniquity, and save me from bloody men." (KJV)

Sin that is not our own can feel like a shroud over our lives, a cloak of darkness, keeping us from seeing Christ and His light. It can feel like the weight of the world is on our chests, physically, mentally, or spiritually.

Dear reader, I am so very sorry if you have suffered because someone else's sin has cut deeply into your life. If you have, I invite you to turn to Psalm 23 and take a few moments to find refuge in Jesus' overflowing love for you described there. Yes—Jesus' reconciliation and restoration mean that one day He will right every wrong.

Paul reminds the Colossians and each of us reading today that Jesus has taken the power out of all the hostility in the world by His death on the cross.

What did Jesus reconcile and how did He reconcile it, according to *Colossians 1:20*?

What did Jesus reconcile and how did He reconcile it, according to *Colossians 1:21–22*? For what purpose?

Christ reconciles us to Himself, through Himself. That's a wild thought! Even though our estrangement from God was our fault because of our sin, even though we had no interest in being reconciled to Him, even though we were still hostile to Him, Christ died the death we deserved for our sinful rebellion and alienation from Him. He came to us and came among us in order to bring us back to Himself. His death and resurrection in our place reconciled our estrangement from Him.

Jesus died to pay the price for every sin, once and for all time. Some people still refuse to be reconciled to God through Jesus. God doesn't force people to love Him or trust Him. So even though Jesus is the only one who can fill the gaping hole in our lives, even though He has done everything to restore and reconcile us to God and one another, sometimes people still reject Jesus' gift and remain hostile toward God.

According to the following passages, what does the reconciliation Jesus accomplished tell us about how God feels about us or looks on us?

Romans 5:6–11

Have you ever wondered, "What in the world is God's plan for my life?" In Colossians 1:21–27, we see where God's master plan touches His plans for each of our lives.

Read Colossians 1:21–27. What changes or curveballs in your life bring up the question, "What is God's plan for me?"

God's plan for us is to be reconciled to Him through Jesus. That was God's plan for the Colossians and for Paul. That's what Paul means when he says:

> The stewardship from God that was given to me for you, to make the word of God fully known, the mystery hidden for ages and generations but now revealed to His saints. (Colossians 1:25–26)

God cares about every part of our lives because He cares for us holistically. However, His plans for our individual lives always fit into His bigger plan of salvation for all people. This means that we have a whole lot of Christian freedom concerning the stuff that does not directly affect our or someone else's salvation and forgiveness.

If you're like me, you might often look at your life and wonder, "Which way should I go?" Paul speaks regularly in the New Testament of following the Spirit. But that does not mean the Holy Spirit is going to reveal to us whether we should go to the grocery store at 2:00 p.m. Instead, God's Word reveals to us all that we need to know about His plans for us—not only His plan for our salvation through the reconciliation Jesus' accomplished, but also His plan for us to reflect Him to the world, living in forgiveness, love, hope, and joy by the Holy Spirit because we are His reconciled people, His saints. His Word doesn't tell us the specifics of what we should do and when we should do it. But the reconciliation Jesus has accomplished for us and for the sake of the whole world is all that we actually need to know in order to make decisions that are within God's will.

God's plans operate like an umbrella, with the bigger, wider curves being paramount to how we understand and see what God wants or wills for our lives.

Sin is never the path God chooses for us, because God hates sin; but beyond that, He gives us immense freedom in the decisions we make. It's a gift!

In most cases, we could turn to the right or to the left, and God would bless either decision, because they both fit within the umbrella of our salvation and the salvation of mankind. When we want someone to help guide us in a decision, God often works through people in the community that is the Church to help us discern our decisions within the bigger umbrellas.

The result of Christ's reconciliation is not anxiety about what to do or how to live, but rather freedom as we live in the relationship Christ has given us with Himself. As Paul wrote to another group of believers,

For freedom Christ has set us free; stand firm therefore, and do not submit again to a yoke of slavery. (Galatians 5:1)

The false teachers in Colossae wanted to rob the believers there of freedom by saying they needed something more than Christ's reconciliation. We, too, struggle to let Christ's reconciliation be all that we need—needing nothing more and nothing less—and living in the freedom it gives. So we keep returning to His Word, to verses like Colossians 1:26–27. The mystery that we need to know has been "revealed to His saints," that is, to us, you and me who are made holy in Jesus. He has turned our hostility toward God into an authentic and intimate relationship. Even though much of God's work is still a mystery to us, His Word reveals that no matter what else happens, we are always under the gracious umbrella of our mighty and mysterious Savior, whom we call Lord.

What kind of day-to-day life plans do you wish God would weigh in on for your life at this moment?

What comfort is there in knowing that God gives freedom in our decisions beneath the umbrella of His salvation won for us by Jesus Christ?

Be assured and comforted that our mighty and mysterious Savior, who reconciles us to Himself, also surely works in our lives every day.

Connected by the Word

Use the Scripture memory verse for the week and the prayer prompt to bring your confession, thanksgiving, praise, and requests before our mighty and mysterious God.

Week 2 Memory Verse

And He is before all things, and in Him all things hold together. (Colossians 1:17)

Prayer Prompt

Lord, there are times when I've been hostile toward You in the past. And there are times even now that I struggle against You and Your plans for me. Today I ask You to renew my heart to have assurance in You, no matter what life may bring . . .

Day 5

KNITTER OF ALL
COLOSSIANS 1:27–2:3

Friendships are fun and good. They make life more enjoyable, struggle more palatable, and everyday events a touch more festive. Friendship is a beautiful gift from God, but we would be fooling ourselves to believe making friends is easy, or that keeping friends is any easier. Intimacy takes time and energy, a lot of mercy, some confession, and more than a little sprinkling of love.

Friendship is also a deep need. I have heard arguments to the contrary, and while some of us might need fewer friendships than other people need, we do all need deep and meaningful relationships of some kind in our lives. As a therapist, I hear from lots of people searching for friends. As a deaconess, I hear from people searching for friends. As a neighbor, I hear from people searching for friends. We, as people on this planet, want to be connected in some way with someone.

Those of us who know Jesus also know a secret. It's time to let the world in on this secret. This secret changes how we make and form friendships, how we see ourselves, how we endure hard things in life, and where we land when we come down from the mountaintops of life. What is this great, big secret?

RELATIONSHIPS WORK BEST WHEN THEY ARE ABOUT SOMETHING GREATER THAN US.

The best place to learn about making authentic relationships, according to Scripture, is the *Church*.

I lose about half the readers on my blog when I say the word *church*.

There are people who have been hurt by *church*.

There are people who see the *church* as empty rituals bringing only complacency.

There are people who have never met a *church* that is interested in them or their lives.

FRIENDSHIP, RELATIONSHIPS, AND THE CHURCH
John 15:12–17

1 Corinthians 12:12–26

Colossians 3:12–14

CHURCH, LIKE FRIENDSHIP, CAN BE HARD.

2 Timothy 3:16–17
"All Scripture is breathed out by God and profitable for teaching, for reproof, for correction, and for training in righteousness, that the man of God may be complete, equipped for every good work."

Let's first gain a firm understanding of what church is and where it comes from before we further explain how the church shows us what true relationships look like. God's Word is the essential place to start—because it's *God's* Word, inspired by the Holy Spirit, not just a collection of human ideas.

Paul wrote a lot about the Body of Christ because he loved it, even while he was completely aware of its warts and wounds. He sought to help the Colossians wrestle with the question, "What is the Church? How is it the Body, the community, of Christ, even though it's so flawed?" We, too, can come to God with our wrestling over the same questions and let Him speak His perfect truth into our world. One place Paul writes about the Body of Christ is Colossians 1:27–2:3. Because he doesn't overtly use the word *church* in this section, it can be easy to miss its application to the church. It's helpful to pan out and remember the context of these verses. Fill in the missing words of Colossians 1:24 below to see a broader vision for today's segment:

Now I rejoice in my sufferings for your sake, and in my flesh I am filling up what is lacking in Christ's afflictions for the sake of _____ _____ , that is, _____ _____ .

Now read Colossians 1:24–2:3. What are some of the characteristics of the Body of Christ that you see in this section?

Laodicea
It is likely Paul mentions the Christians in Laodicea here because the churches in Colossae, Laodicea, and another town, Hierapolis, were like a tripoint parish or sister congregations. You can see how close in proximity these cities were on the map on page 14.

Look again at Colossians 1:27–2:3 and write down in the chart below as much as you can about what this section says about these relationships.

Christ's Relationship to the Church	Relationships within the Church
God reveals things through His Word taught, preached, and studied.	We share God's Word with one another and within our communities together.

88

Christ's Relationship to the Church

The Church was God's idea—not Paul's, not Timothy's, not your pastor's, not your grandparents', not the Pope's, not the reformers', nor anyone else's. This gig is Christ's alone, just as we are created and saved by Christ alone. As we said two days ago, Jesus is the head of the Church, and as we said yesterday, He is the reconciler of the Church to God the Father. In a very succinct way, 1 Corinthians 1:2 helps us understand the relationship between Christ and the Church. Circle words or phrases that describe the Church in that verse below:

To the church of God that is in Corinth, to those sanctified in Christ Jesus, called to be saints together with all those who in every place call upon the name of our Lord Jesus Christ, both their Lord and ours. (1 Corinthians 1:2)

Jesus is the Lord of the Church. He calls people into His Church, and He sanctifies them. That means those in the Church are not defined by who they are on their own; rather, they are defined by who Christ causes them to be. He reconciles them not only to God but also to one another and makes them holy in Him. This holiness, this set-apart quality, makes it possible for His Church to be called the sainthood of all believers, even when the people in the Church appear to be less than perfect saints by common standards.

> **1 PETER 2:5, 9**
> "You yourselves like living stones are being built up as a spiritual house, to be a holy priesthood, to offer spiritual sacrifices acceptable to God through Jesus Christ. . . . But you are a chosen race, a royal priesthood, a holy nation, a people for His own possession, that you may proclaim the excellencies of Him who called you out of darkness into His marvelous light."

Relationships within the Church

As Colossians 2:2 says, Jesus knits the sainthood of all believers together in love. It's not just "me and Jesus." When I am in Christ, I am in Christ with others. Jesus binds us to one another inseparably through His love. Giant, gaping holes in our relationships are the reality in this sin-infected world. Jesus' knitting us together also means He mends our relationships. It reminds me of mending holes ripped open in little boys' pant knees. In the Church, Jesus is the strong thread that sews people together and mends relationships. Wrongs and hurts can be forgiven and healed because His love for us is so great. His love binds us together when nothing else is strong enough. He creates relationships that are stronger than any we could have ever had without all the mending and sewing.

Whom does God invite to be a part of His Church, according to Colossians 1:28?

Those promoting false teaching among the Colossians wanted only certain people to be invited into the Church. Paul reminds them and us that Christ operates differently. Our God wants everyone, always. These truths about Christ's relationship with His Church change the way we interact with one another.

God's Created Design Restored within the Church

We were not created to exist as islands. Just as God created us to need food, water, and shelter, He created us to need connection with other people. While God has always known our need, research in the past few years has started identifying that a lack of connection is indeed a primary component that contributes to addiction, self-harm, and violence.[12]

WE ARE PEOPLE WHO NEED GOD, WHETHER WE KNOW IT OR NOT.

AND WE ARE PEOPLE WHO NEED PEOPLE, WHETHER WE KNOW IT OR NOT.

In Genesis 2:25, what two characteristics did Adam and Eve enjoy with God and each other before sin entered the picture?

Genesis 2:25 is more than a verse only about God's intention for marriage relationships. Rather, it's a lens into the way God intended all relationships in His creation to be. Sin corrupted what God created, and as a result, intimacy and selflessness are nearly impossible for us. But Christ re-creates what was tainted and broken by sin.

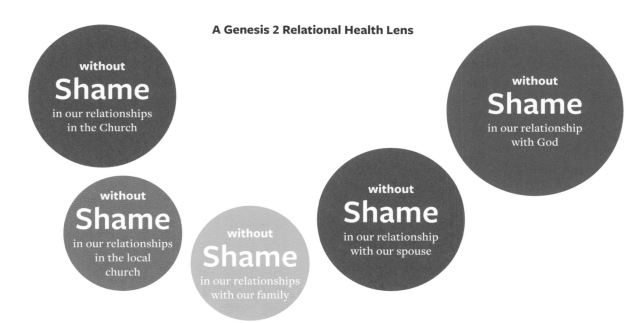

A Genesis 2 Relational Health Lens

without **Shame** in our relationships in the Church

without **Shame** in our relationships in the local church

without **Shame** in our relationships with our family

without **Shame** in our relationship with our spouse

without **Shame** in our relationship with God

GRAPHIC COPYRIGHT © HEIDI GOEHMANN

First, Christ shows us through His love and forgiveness that we are absolutely safe with Him and in Him. We are naked and unashamed emotionally and relationally with God because we are known by Christ.

Because of the love, forgiveness, and absolute security Jesus gives us, we experience an emotional and relational safety in our homes when Jesus is the center of our marriages and families, which is impossible without His grace and redemption. The mystery of a Christian marriage reflects the naked and unashamed intimacy God gives us with Himself in Christ. We share this safety and intimacy with the children we raise in our homes.

And God also gives us the community of the family of believers—our brothers and sisters in Christ—and there, too, He gives the gift of being able to be naked and unashamed with one another because we are Christ's Body, the Church. Authentic life together is part of being a unified Body.

Of course, we aren't going around living in a naked-and-unashamed community physically; but emotionally and relationally, the idea of being naked and unashamed changes the way we communicate and connect with one another. We get to be ourselves in the Church. The Church is the place we learn to see ourselves and others as we truly are: forgiven, beloved, perfect, and holy children of God.

The layers of relationships Christ knits together in our lives are safer, more powerful, more beautiful than anything this world could offer us. Sin will still infiltrate; it will still reside in the imperfect church, our imperfect homes, and our imperfect friendships until Christ returns. But all of our relationships exist in a bigger picture, a broader plan of the perfect and triumphant Church Christ will usher in when He comes back for us. There, in eternity, we will know what the safety of naked and unashamed looked like for Adam and Eve in the garden, and we will be His new creation forever, joyfully gathered together and with Him.

I know some days it feels like we're waiting for a pipe dream: a day when there are no more tears, when evil is trampled, and when we are safe and secure forever. Our relationships now and the Church on earth as we see it are imperfect, but they are still gifts from God, which means we don't want to give up on them. Christ's mercy and forgiveness and reconciliation permeates His Church by the Holy Spirit and re-creates God's creation even now, giving glimpses of what we will see in full when He returns.

In Colossians 1:29–2:1, which words convey that giving love and care within the community of the church is hard work?

Paul calls it toiling for a reason. This isn't a toiling unique to Paul as a pastor or evangelist. This is the toiling of all believers—a toiling to live life in the community of the Church, sharing the Gospel together, for His kingdom, His glory.

When Paul says this is a "struggle," his language indicates that this is a struggle against difficult opposition. This toiling and struggling is going to take all the energy we can muster. It might almost get the better of us or make us call uncle. This toil and struggle of relationship is deep, exhausting, and tiring. But it's worth it. And it is one of the trademarks of God's people in Christ.

Have you had experiences in the church that remind you how difficult it is to have deep, intimate, naked-and-unashamed relationships?

Have you had relationships in the church that remind you how worthwhile these deep, intimate, naked-and-unashamed relationships can be?

What comes with these close-knit, naked-and-unashamed relationships within the imperfect but beautiful Body of Christ, according to Colossians 2:2–3?

ESCHATOLOGY
The study of the end times; particularly, the study of how God will resolve the brokenness of the world and will usher in the new creation when Jesus returns.

The fact that Paul can feel and write this way toward Christians he had never met (2:1) shows how relationships in the Body of Christ go beyond simple friendship. The world wants friendship; but what they don't know is that the most intimate, authentic relationships can only come in Christ. Because He redeems what is broken. No matter how messed up the Church on earth is, it knows intimacy mysteriously, because it is a work of Christ's knitting. God is the one in charge of the Church and each relationship in the Church, sustaining, re-creating, and providing. I want to be part of that.

Though the Church is not immune to the challenges of relationships, I would rather be knit into Christ's Body by this mighty and mysterious God than go at this world alone, lonely and afraid. Today remember that you are found in every way—safe and unashamed in the arms of Christ.

Connected by the Word

Use the Scripture memory verse for the week and the prayer prompt to bring your confession, thanksgiving, praise, and requests before our mighty and mysterious God.

Week 2 Memory Verse

And He is before all things, and in Him all things hold together. (Colossians 1:17)

Prayer Prompt

Savior, You are the master knitter. Today I am thankful that You have intimately connected me to You, my Redeemer and Friend. I am also thankful for all those You knit into my life . . .

Week 3
ALL THAT IS MYSTERIOUS

Viewer Guide

VIDEO 3: ON DRAMA AND HERESY
COLOSSIANS 2:4–23

> **Real Drama:** When God's Word and the Gospel are unclear.

> **Drama Making:** When people say certain rules or actions are required in order to be a Christian.

JOHN 14:6–7
"I am the way, and the truth, and the life. No one comes to the Father except through Me. If you had known Me, you would have known My Father also. From now on you do know Him and have seen Him."

The word *heresy* assumes that there is such a thing as truth.
SEE COLOSSIANS 2:4–10.

Heresy, by nature, is always an addition to or an opposition to the Gospel of Christ.

Paul and Timothy respond by proclaiming again, clearly and powerfully, who Jesus is.

HERESY
A teaching, belief, theory, or opinion that is contrary to what Scripture teaches. A broad definition of *heresy* can be any teachings, beliefs, theories, or opinions that are against an established custom or religious belief. But for the purposes of our study, we will use the narrower definition of *heresy* as anything that is contrary to the teachings in the Bible.

FALSE TEACHING 1: PHILOSOPHICAL

1. According to _____ _____

2. According to _____ _____ _____ _____ _____

   _____

3. *NOT* according to _____
SEE COLOSSIANS 2:18.

EPHESIANS 4:4–6
"There is one body and one Spirit—just as you were called to the one hope that belongs to your call—one Lord, one faith, one baptism, one God and Father of all, who is over all and through all and in all."

FALSE TEACHING 2: RITUALISTIC

SEE COLOSSIANS 2:20–23.

Anything that proclaims, "Look at me!" explicitly or implicitly _____ attention from Christ.

BUT . . .

Jesus came to save us from our desire to find false _____ in rituals.

SEE COLOSSIANS 2:10.

FALSE TEACHING 3: FUSION

If it jeopardizes what _____ says, then we can't accept it; it can't be fused with our _____.

DISCUSSION QUESTIONS

1. When have you seen or heard false teachings or disagreement dealt with well? When have you seen or heard false teaching or disagreement dealt with poorly, and how does that stir up unnecessary drama?

2. With which topics of faith are people most often tempted to let logic control God's Word? Why does human logic break down when we try to reason about our faith? What place does human logic or reason have in relationship to our faith?

3. Which of the three aspects of the Colossian heresy most reflects your own tendencies? In light of that tendency, who in your life helps you to discern truth and falsehood?

THE COLOSSIAN HERESY
A collection of false teachings among the Christians in Colossae. Some of these teachings included the need to worship a pantheon of spirits in addition to worshiping Jesus; restrictions or requirements concerning rituals, feast days, and special celebrations; and the need to obtain higher, special knowledge about God beyond the Gospel of Jesus in order to become closer to God.

1 JOHN 4:4
"Little children, you are from God and have overcome them, for He who is in you is greater than he who is in the world."

AUTHOR'S NOTE
We tend to hear truth as law, as something that shows us our sin, because it's often hard for us to accept that God's truth is absolutely true, beyond our own truth. But Christ wraps even our struggle with God's truth in His grace and forgiveness. He also brings us to see that His truth is actually Good News. The one big Gospel truth is that Jesus is enough. He died and rose for us. That is the truth that is true beyond anything else we could ever know. And that truth changes everything.

Day 1

HIDDEN TREASURES
COLOSSIANS 2:1–3

In November, I went shopping. I peeled off the price tags and carefully wrapped each find with fabric and ribbon. I placed the wrapped packages under our Christmas tree and waited. It took all of twenty minutes before one of my children walked over to the tree and investigated the situation. Pretty soon, all of our children were all over those presents. They would pick up one package and then set it back down. They crouched down and touched their noses to the heavy packages they couldn't lift to see the name of the recipient. They contorted their bodies to get glimpses of the presents tucked behind the tree. It was so fun to watch because of their curiosity and joy. Sure, they would have enjoyed ripping into the packages right then and there. But simply knowing gifts were waiting for them, hidden beneath all the wrappings and trimmings, was enough to fill them with joyful anticipation and glee. They didn't need to open the packages to find joy. And in fact, I think their joy on Christmas morning when they opened their packages was stronger because they had spent time anticipating the hidden treasures waiting for them inside the packages they could see.

As Christians, we are like children waiting for Christmas morning. We are waiting for all the hidden treasures of our faith to be revealed. Jesus is our Savior now, no less today than He will be when we finally see Him face-to-face. His Word and His presence with us through our Baptism and through the Lord's Supper are what we can see now. They are like the packages under the Christmas tree in this way: they give us joy now because they testify to the gift—Jesus, our Savior, and His love. But we long to see the gift fully. So, God's Word and Sacraments also give us joy because they testify and point ahead to what is still to come—what is hidden that will be fully revealed one day soon. On that day, when Jesus comes again, we will see fully who He is *over all*, and we will also see all of the treasures currently hidden in Jesus be "unwrapped."

Then our joy will be uncontainable and will flow like a river running wild. It will be our Christmas morning.

In Colossians 2:1–3, Paul talks about these treasures we have in Christ now and the hidden treasures in Him yet to come.

Fill in the blanks within Colossians 2:1–3 below:

For I want you to know how great a struggle I have for you and for those at Laodicea and for all who have not seen me face to face, that their hearts may be encouraged, being knit together in love, to reach _____ _____ _____ of full assurance of understanding and the knowledge of God's mystery, which is Christ, in whom are hidden _____ _____ _____ of wisdom and knowledge.

What images or other descriptions come to mind when you hear those two phrases you just filled in?

There's something I don't want you to miss. Underline or highlight the name *Christ* in the verses above. Now circle the tiny verb that comes before it.

Paul uses the word *mystery* four times in his Letter to the Colossians, and he talks about concepts that are difficult to understand and can seem "mysterious" plenty more than four times. But in these verses, Paul tells us that the mystery *is* Christ. Christ—His death and resurrection for the salvation and reconciliation of the whole world, and His love for all people—is the mystery that had been hidden for all the years before Jesus became man and came among us. And now God's grace has revealed this mystery to us. In Christ Jesus, we know all that is mysterious that we need to know. This is a beautiful gift for every believer. To those who do not have Christ, the treasures of wisdom and knowledge are still hidden. But those who believe in Christ have

COLOSSIANS 1:26
"The mystery hidden for ages and generations but now revealed to His saints."

all the riches of full assurance of understanding and the knowledge of God's mystery (Colossians 2:2)

and

all the treasures of wisdom and knowledge.
(Colossians 2:3)

We have to remember this when we encounter people who don't believe in Jesus and we try to help them trust in Him. Jesus is a mystery who doesn't make any sense to us as human beings until the Holy Spirit opens our eyes and our hearts through God's Word.

What does 1 Corinthians 2:1–16 say about the relationship between having God's Spirit and having the wisdom of God?

AUTHOR'S NOTE
I find the NIV wording of 1 Corinthians 2:13–14 particularly helpful because it shows how the Spirit is the one who imparts knowledge and understanding:

"This is what we speak, not in words taught us by human wisdom but in words taught by the Spirit, explaining spiritual realities with Spirit-taught words. The person without the Spirit does not accept the things that come from the Spirit of God but considers them foolishness, and cannot understand them because they are discerned only through the Spirit." (NIV)

There were false teachers telling the Colossians they needed more knowledge than what is in God's Word—more, special, deeper knowledge than what the Colossians had come to believe through the Holy Spirit: something beyond believing that Jesus, the Son of God, became man, died on the cross for their sins, rose again to give them eternal life, and is coming back to take them to be with Him forever. Paul wanted the Colossians to know, without a doubt, "No, the only treasures of knowledge are in Christ."

God's Word is all we need. It is our only source of the riches of understanding and the treasures of wisdom. And yet we, too, are tempted to want something other than or beyond God's Word.

How many people live disconnected from God's Word? How many people, even within the church, live disconnected from the Word? How often do we turn to everything but the Word to try to understand life or to try to find wisdom? God's Word doesn't always answer all of our questions. But it is the only source of true wisdom. It answers the most important questions—the worldview planks we talked about in Video 1: *Who am I and where did I come from? Do I have a purpose? Where do things and people get their value? Where am I going, and where is the world going?* Through faith in Jesus, we trust that the answers God's Word does give us are enough.

Yet don't forget what we studied on day 5 last week. In the same breath that Paul declares to the Colossians that they have all the riches and treasures of knowledge they could ever need in Christ, he is saying that they have these riches as a knit-together group.

According to Colossians 2:2, how are hearts affected by being knit together in love and having these riches of knowledge in Christ together?

Why is it an encouragement to have the treasures of wisdom and knowledge together, rather than alone?

God does not leave us alone. Not only is He always with us, but He also gives to us other Christians, the fellowship of believers, with whom to share life and rejoice together in God's good gifts.

We love one another because He has loved us—and we see His love in the love we receive from others. We give and receive God's mercy to and from one another because we know one day the final proclamation over each of us who are in Christ will be that we are forgiven and perfect in Christ.

When we look at one another in the Church, by God's grace, we see one another as those who have all the riches of wisdom in Christ. Having wisdom together in Christ means that God often works through other Christians to speak His wisdom and truth into our lives and to encourage us with His Word. When we gather around His Word together, and when we eat and drink together at the Lord's Supper, God knits us with one another and with Himself. And He gives us the fullness of knowledge and understanding in Him together. There aren't any treasures or riches more valuable than Jesus and Jesus acting on our behalf.

Whom has God placed around you, as part of His Church, to be encouraged and knit together?

AUTHOR'S NOTE
Jesus' death and resurrection compared to Jesus coming back again always makes me think of a fireworks show compared to the finale of the same fireworks show. We are saved and blown away now by Jesus' life, death, sacrifice, and victory. Can you even imagine what Jesus coming back for us will be like?

In your prayers today, give thanks for the work of Christ that reveals God and His plan of salvation for us, and then ask God to help you see those who are still longing for true knowledge, wisdom, and understanding—and therefore longing also for hope and mercy.

CONNECTED BY THE WORD

Use the Scripture memory verse for the week and the prayer prompt to bring your confession, thanksgiving, praise, and requests before our mighty and mysterious God.

WEEK 3 MEMORY VERSE

In whom are hidden all the treasures of wisdom and knowledge. (Colossians 2:3)

PRAYER PROMPT

Savior, You are the mystery, and in You, we have all the wisdom and understanding we need. Thank You! Lord, today I pray for those who may be lost, without knowledge of You . . .

Day 2

ASKING QUESTIONS, KEEPING BALANCE
COLOSSIANS 2:4–5

My husband and I have a small obsession with the BBC television series *Sherlock*, which began airing in 2010. It is a modern take on Arthur Conan Doyle's famous works of literature. I watch this particular series for its cinematography, strong characters, and unique twists on a beloved piece of classic literature. My husband . . . he's really there for the whodunit. His brain loves the mystery—following the trail from start to finish, assembling the pieces of the puzzle one at a time, slowly at first and then in rapid fire. He likes the anticipation of the aha moment. When the anticipation of the aha moment reaches the point of frenzy, *I* grab a book, hide behind it, and peek out occasionally at the TV screen to keep my anxiety from boiling over. The show captivates our attention because it brings to the surface a million questions, but then answers all of them—all within ninety minutes.

Asking questions is something we as human beings start doing when we're very young. It's how children learn about their world. As adults, we don't lose the natural tendency to ask questions, even if we speak fewer of our questions aloud. Fictional stories, television shows, and movie characters in particular often rouse our curiosity and our questions: How did this come about? Why is that person acting like that? What is the relationship between these people? Is there a way to fix the situation? The same thing happens when we are introduced to a new person in real life and his or her story. Our minds start asking questions: Where is this person from? What is her family like? What does he do for fun? Why would she want to do that for a living?

Some of us enjoy discussing big-picture questions—like philosophical questions of whether the chicken or the egg came first, or whether a tree makes a sound when it falls if no one hears it—or questions of politics, ethics, morality, sociology, or psychology.

Do you enjoy discussing big-picture questions? If so, what questions do you find yourself coming back to? If not, can you describe why you don't like discussing such questions?

As we talked about in Video 1 and mentioned in yesterday's study, there are some questions in life that are really important—the worldview questions. Sometimes we aren't even aware that we are asking these questions or living by particular answers to them. Consider these:

- Who am I?
- Where did I come from?
- What is my purpose? What is God's will for me?
- Am I lovable? Am I valuable?
- What happens when we die?

The Colossians were asking a lot of questions about who Jesus is and what He has done—and the answers to those questions affected the Colossians' answers to their worldview questions about themselves. People in our world generally don't ask many direct questions about Jesus. But by people's answers to their worldview questions, they are living with particular answers about Jesus as well, whether they realize it or not.

Much of our life revolves around these questions and whom we let answer them—God or other people.

Open your Bible to Colossians 2:4. What is Paul's concern as the Colossians ask questions?

Look through the questions I list below. Choose two or three and write next to them ways people can be deluded, or misled, when discussing or answering those questions:

Who am I?

Where did I come from?

What is my purpose or what is God's will for me?

Am I lovable, valuable?

What happens when we die?

We are misled when we let other people answer the worldview questions that only God is supposed to answer.

παραλογίζομαι
paralogizomai: to mislead.[21]

When we hear the word "delude" or "mislead," we might assume the false teachers at Colossae were out to harm the new believers. But in actuality, the Greek word in Colossians 2:4 translated as "delude" or "deceive" does not necessarily imply a dark or ulterior motive. The false teachers may very well have sincerely thought they were helping the Colossians. Sometimes people do intend evil. But more often, we encounter deception that sounds plausible because people—even our friends—try to help but end up offering terrible advice.

Describe a time you encountered someone who gave bad advice or teachings, but truly thought they were being helpful.

In Colossians 2:4, Paul says one of the reasons he has been writing to the Colossians about the riches they have in Christ is so that they hold to Jesus' truth, rather than listen to what the false teachers have been telling them.

According to Paul in Colossians 2:5, what helps those in the Church combat deceptively plausible arguments?

God is a God of order. He brings order to our families with husbands loving wives, wives respecting husbands, mothers and fathers taking care of children, and then those children growing up and leaving their parents to cleave to a spouse. God brings order to society with necessary hierarchies like government, civil authorities, and systems that bring justice and protect those who cannot protect themselves. God also gives order to the community of those who believe in Jesus by giving us the Church. The Church is imperfect until Jesus comes again, but nevertheless it is a structure of society designed, not by man, but by God Himself.

How does the Church bring order to our individual and communal walks of faith?

Congregations in God's Church will not always feel like God's gift of good order to you. If you haven't already experienced that, you probably will at some point. Perhaps you're experiencing it now. Perhaps you exist disconnected from a local body of believers because you recently moved. Maybe you never grew up going to church, and though you believe in Jesus, it's intimidating and uncomfortable to try to connect with a church near you. Maybe you have been part of the same congregation for many years, but it has changed and you miss the way things used to be, so now you don't feel comfortable there anymore. Maybe you have so much going on with your family and your work and other commitments that you don't have time to invest in a local community of Christians or have become distant from a local faith community you once knew. Maybe you have been hurt by those in the Church, those who were supposed to love you best, and now you want nothing to do with any local part of the Church. All of these circumstances make sense and are very real. This life together as a community of faith is really hard. In fact, if we are doing it authentically, with real investment, actually knowing one another, being part of one another's day-to-day life, and spending some meaningful time together, it will be one of the hardest things we have ever done.

Whether we are part of a local congregation or not, we all struggle with connecting authentically to those in a local congregation. It may be difficult to be honest with yourself about this, but what keeps you from diving more intimately into a local manifestation of the larger Body of Christ at present?

Name at least one thing people miss out on if they are disconnected from the local church.

The order of the church might include traditions, leadership, organization, buildings, and policies. It is easy to make too much or too little of these things.

What do you think adds to good order in the life of the church body? What seems needless to you for good order?

I wish I could see your answers to those hard questions and pray over them with you. Because the Church is broken (like all of us who are part of it), it is very hard to swallow that we *need* the Church. Being a part of the good order of the Church in its local, everyday life ways, having relationships with those in the Church, and letting ourselves be known by those in the Church can be some of the greatest challenges of the Christian walk.

And yet Paul tells the Colossians that having good order in the Church is very important so that we can avoid being deluded by plausible arguments. How is this true? Because living together in Christ allows us to be balanced out by one another.

When those who are in Christ look to God's Word first, when they bring their worldview questions to the Scriptures, they search the Scriptures together and discuss and listen to one another as they wrestle to understand what the Scriptures say. The Holy Spirit guides them and balances out the bias of any one human opinion of what God says with what others in the Church understand God's Word to be saying. Paul encourages the Colossians to continue in their good order by continuing to search the Scriptures together, continuously looking to what God says as they seek to answer the hard questions about faith, about Jesus, and about the Christian life. Paul commends not just any semblance of order, but rather order that is truly *good*—order that strives to live as God intended—because it points clearly to Christ, fostering firm faith in Him.

Below I've brainstormed some things that I struggle to balance in my Christian walk. If you can relate to any of these, next to those pairs write your thoughts about why it's difficult to hold both things in balance. Add any other pairs you can think of in the blank space on the next page.

Law and Gospel

Sinner and saint

Saved and still growing

Faith and reason

Paul also spoke to the Corinthian Church quite a bit about order. They were having a hard time figuring out what was order and what was disorder. Paul did not want deception to spread among them either. In a chapter all about how the Corinthians were worshiping, prophesying, and speaking in tongues, Paul gives exhortation for balance:

When you come together, each one has a hymn, a lesson, a revelation, a tongue, or an interpretation. Let all things be done for building up. If any speak in a tongue, let there be only two or at most three, and each in turn, and let someone interpret. But if there is no one to interpret, let each of them keep silent in church and speak to himself and to God. Let two or three prophets speak, and let the others weigh what is said. If a revelation is made to another sitting there, let the first be silent. For you can all prophesy one by one, so that all may learn and all be encouraged, and the spirits of prophets are subject to prophets. For God is not a God of confusion but of peace. . . . All things should be done decently and in order.

(1 Corinthians 14:26–33, 40)

Order is bringing the Word to one another in a way that makes sense. If I'm not making sense to my fellow Christians, I am not building up. Therefore, what I'm saying is likely in the category of plausible arguments. When God's Word is present, when it builds us up together, when it comes among us and creates real relationships rooted in firmness of faith in Christ, that's the Spirit at work, a balance of order. In 1 Corinthians 14:33, Paul gives some balm for our question-weary, balance-struggling souls.

Write the first sentence of 1 Corinthians 14:33 below.

Jesus is the one who gives truth rather than plausible arguments. Jesus is the one who holds the answers to all of our questions. Jesus is the one who brings us together in community and gives balance, providing order as we ask questions and study God's Word together.

EVEN AMONGST ALL OF LIFE'S QUESTIONS, HE IS A GOD NOT OF CONFUSION, BUT OF PEACE.

CONNECTED BY THE WORD

Use the Scripture memory verse for the week and the prayer prompt to bring your confession, thanksgiving, praise, and requests before our mighty and mysterious God.

WEEK 3 MEMORY VERSE

In whom are hidden all the treasures of wisdom and knowledge. (Colossians 2:3)

PRAYER PROMPT

Lord, I have many questions. The answers I need are in Christ. Help me to live by the answers You give, and to live in the good order You give in the Church, even when it's hard . . .

Day 3

THE MYSTERIOUS WALK
COLOSSIANS 2:6–7

I was baptized on Mother's Day, 1979. My mama always reminded me I was a gift from God. She picked Mother's Day, three weeks after my birth, as my Baptism birthday not idly, but as intentional thanksgiving for an unexpected baby at just the right time. What she didn't know then was that within eighteen months, she would be a single mom, trudging through a walk of grief she couldn't have imagined and would never have chosen for herself. She would need to lean heavily on the promises the Spirit of the living God spoke over me on that Mother's Day in 1979.

Our journeys on this earth hold at least a little of the unexpected. What have you walked through during your life that was unexpected to you?

Our journeys also hold at least a little of what makes life hard—grief, pain, fear, and change. What have you walked through in your life that has been painful or hard, even if you came out better on the other side?

In our short snippet of Colossians today, the authors encourage the Colossians to keep walking with Christ.

Open your Bible to Colossians 2:6–7. How is the Christian walk described in these two verses?

One gift of our Baptism is that we can look at it, remember the day, the instance, the moment, and have complete confidence that we have received

Christ in our hearts and lives. The life we then have in Christ could be described in many ways: the freedom of driving on the open road, with the windows down and hair blowing in the breeze; the confidence of standing up tall because we know who we are and where we're going; the peace of a warm cup of tea as we watch snow fall. But here Paul chooses to describe the life we have in Christ as a walk. Walking makes us think of movement and exercise, but for New Testament hearers, the image of walking was also closely connected to journeying.

Colossians 2:6 mentions two different, though related, journeys:

Therefore, as you received Christ Jesus the Lord — *the salvation pilgrimage*

so walk in Him. — *the daily pilgrimage*

Pilgrimage is a fancy word for "journey." But it fits well when we talk about journeying with Jesus. A pilgrim is a worshiper, a devotee, a follower. Through our Baptism, Christ invites us into His family and tells us who we are in Him. Our *salvation pilgrimage* is completed right then and there, at our Baptism. We *received* Christ—past tense. He saved us and took us safely through the waters to the end of our salvation journey.

But Paul encourages the Colossians and us to also walk in our daily lives with Christ. It is a *daily pilgrimage* because we follow our Savior on this daily journey. We worship Him through every step, at every bend in the road, and we remain devoted to Him, connected to the One who gave us our identity.

No analogy is perfect, but an image I often think of concerning our Christian journeys is that of a passport. In this analogy, our Baptism is like our passport on our daily pilgrimage.

Becoming a passport holder opens doors; it brings unpredictable freedom and adventure, but it also carries risk. A passport proclaims our identity: where we are from, our nationality, and our name. In the same way, our Baptism reminds us that we belong to Jesus and our identity is in Him. A passport opens up opportunities for us to grow—including standing on some mountaintops and wandering through some wildernesses and valleys. So does our Baptism.

If we never used our passport to travel, it would not cease to be a passport, and what the passport says about us would still be true. However, a person obtains a passport for a reason—not just to store it in a drawer.

In the same way, our identity in Christ is secure and does not change based on our actions and movements. But Christ gave us the absolute assurance of this identity in Baptism for a reason: so that He can be our constant companion throughout the daily journey, and so that our daily pilgrimage can reflect the salvation pilgrimage He has already led us on. He gives us the passport of our Baptism because He knows that daily journeying in the midst of this

1 THESSALONIANS 2:12
"We exhorted each one of you and encouraged you and charged you to walk in a manner worthy of God, who calls you into His own kingdom and glory."

world can very easily make us forget who we are—or rather, whose we are and where we come from.

Walking through daily life is not easier because you have a passport clarifying your identity in Christ. The pilgrimage is still a challenging journey, full of pit stops and time changes and unexpected circumstances. But this passport does give us an otherworldly freedom as we journey. The salvation pilgrimage that Christ has already completed for us by His death and resurrection gives purpose and peace to our daily pilgrimage. We know securely where our journey ultimately ends, and we know without a doubt that we will make it to this final destination. Now, instead of expending our energy by wondering about our worth and trying to prove our value and protect our resources and future, we are free to focus on growing and connecting with others. We can spend time concerning ourselves with other people's well-being so that they, too, might see the One who alone gives security and purpose in life.

We can look at the daily walk with Jesus Christ truly as an adventure. We often don't know where we are going in the next few weeks or years of our lives. We certainly don't know what we'll experience along the way in life. There will be plenty of ups and downs that we can't prepare for. But whether it is during an up or a down, a mountain or a valley, Christ walks with us on this daily pilgrimage, all the way. He isn't leading us on a journey to find the best beaches or to make sure we check stuff off our bucket list. Sometimes Jesus does give those kinds of things too, but Jesus cares about other adventures more. Like the people He might put in our lives whom we never expected. Or the challenges He might call us to that we don't feel equipped for. Every movement in our daily pilgrimage is purposeful, simply because He is present in the walk. And our passport—reminding us who we are in Christ—doesn't change.

We might think of the unique places and spaces Jesus invites us to share in this life with Him as stamps in our passport.

What do the passport stamps Jesus has given you look like? These might be actual places He has brought you—for me, that would include Missouri, India, Ohio, Haiti, Spain, Nebraska—or people you have shared life with, or both. In the space below, write about some of the experiences, relationships, or places Christ has put in your life on this journey.

One of the stamps in my passport is Haiti. It felt like God moved mountains to make it possible for us to do missionary work there. But within two months of arriving there, our family had an exorbitant amount of health issues. Our grand plans were suddenly cut short. There was weeping. There may have been some gnashing as well. Five years later, I still can't say about that time, "I see where Christ was working. Right there, I see His plans unfolding." If you've ever been through a natural disaster, experienced loss of any kind, or had a dream bite the dust, you might be able to relate. Maybe there is something good God brought *from it*, but still you might be uncertain about where God was *in it*. This is why walking in Christ and walking with Him is a mysterious walk. And this is where the description in Colossians 2:7 of our walk in Christ comes in very handy.

Look up the verses listed with each word from Colossians 2:7 below. Identify how these other verses can help us understand the broader themes in Scripture associated with these images.

Rooted

Revelation 22:16; Revelation 5:5; Ephesians 3:16–19

Built up

Isaiah 44:24–28; Jeremiah 31:2–4; Ephesians 2:19–22

Established

2 Corinthians 1:20–22; 2 Thessalonians 3:3

Taught

Hosea 11:3–4; 2 Timothy 3:10–15; 1 Thessalonians 4:9–10

EPHRAIM
The mention of "Ephraim" in Hosea 11:3 may be a bit confusing. Ephraim was the second son of the patriarch Joseph (the Joseph who was sold into slavery by his brothers and eventually became a ruler of Egypt). Ephraim's descendants became one of the most powerful tribes among the twelve tribes of Israel. So the name *Ephraim* is sometimes used as a synonym for *Israel*—that is, the people of God—in the Bible (notice the connection between Hosea 11:1–2 and Hosea 11:3–4).

ABOUNDING

Exodus 34:6; Romans 5:15; Philippians 4:12–13

FUN ACTIVITY
We abound in so many ways because of Christ! Make a gratitude list today to remind yourself of some of the things God has abundantly provided for you in your daily pilgrimage of life.

The words "rooted . . . built up . . . and established" give the image of a foundation, standing on a solid base. It might sound a little funny to hear images of being securely planted and firmly put in place as descriptions of walking in Christ. But that's precisely what Paul says! Our foundation as we walk is secure on this daily pilgrimage, no matter how mysterious the walking itself can be. Therefore, we are able to abound in thanksgiving as we walk in Him, whether we encounter smooth blacktops or rocky crags ahead.

Jesus is our strong foundation. Jesus establishes us in Him, builds us up in Him, and roots us in Him. As we walk, we worship Him, and He works in us and through us. As we walk, He is doing the mighty and the mysterious in our hearts and in our lives and with our days. No matter what stamps He puts in our passport, He walks with us, all the way.

CONNECTED BY THE WORD

Use the Scripture memory verse for the week and the prayer prompt to bring your confession, thanksgiving, praise, and requests before our mighty and mysterious God.

WEEK 3 MEMORY VERSE

In whom are hidden all the treasures of wisdom and knowledge. (Colossians 2:3)

PRAYER PROMPT

Lord, I know You are not only with me on this journey but also working in me, every step along the way. Some parts of this journey seem exciting and others seem mysterious to me, Lord. Today I ask Your guidance for these things in my daily pilgrimage . . .

Day 4

MYSTERIOUSLY FULL
COLOSSIANS 2:8–14

We live in a culture of lack. We are constantly reminded, by the words from our own mouths or those around us, that there is not enough time, not enough money, not enough energy . . . just not enough. Period.

What are the laments of lack you hear most often—time, money, energy, or something else?

Whether you live in a house with toddlers or teenagers, whether you work at home or in an office, whether you get your news from the TV, the internet, or the grapevine, we all are exposed to and probably infected by what researchers and sociologists commonly call a mind-set of scarcity. However, this is not a new phenomenon. The Colossians also struggled with a mind-set of scarcity.

What do Paul and Timothy say in Colossians 2:8–14 that suggests the Colossian Christians thought what they already had in their relationship with Christ was not "enough"?

We all have a need for fullness and wholeness. What does Ecclesiastes 3:11 say God has knit deeply into each of us?

Eternity is the time when all things will be full, whole, and complete in Jesus Christ. That's what we are all seeking, though we often have a hard time putting our finger on it because our sin has completely tainted and twisted our ability to see things clearly.

True fullness can only be found in whom, according to Colossians 2:8–10?

What are some things people use to try to achieve completeness or wholeness, instead of Jesus?

Paul warns the Colossians not to be taken captive and deceived into thinking something else can give fullness other than Jesus. What threatened to deceive the Colossians and what threatens to deceive us are philosophies that are according to human wisdom, rather than the wisdom of God.

Everything we say and do reflects a philosophy. How many times have you seen a house decoration that says "Live, Laugh, Love"? There's a philosophy in that. How many times has a friend talked about the way someone else or an organization should do something? There's a philosophy in there. How many times have you struggled to make your parents, your spouse, your co-workers, your friend understand your perspective? That's where philosophies bump into one another in our everyday life.

Can you think of a recent example of this in your experience? What philosophy, belief, or mind-set was behind the opinions you heard or actions you saw?

What are some of the philosophies you hear most often or you see people living according to most often in our world?

We often think if we just find the right philosophy or way of doing things, life will be simpler and easier and will go the way we want. Others are quick to affirm that satisfaction and fulfillment come from choosing our own philosophy to live by. But the truth is that human philosophies are incapable of giving the wholeness and fullness we seek because they originate with human beings. Only in Christ can real fullness and meaning be found. However, even those who have Christ—including the Colossians and us—can be enticed to think that we still lack something in Christ and that we need something more than or other than Christ alone.

You may have noticed that Colossians 2:11–13 seems to suggest the Colossians were tempted to think they needed circumcision as well as Christ. If you read on to Colossians 2:16–18, what else does it seem the Colossians were being enticed to think they needed besides Christ?

What are we, as modern-day Christians, enticed to think we need besides Christ?

JOHN 1:16
"For from His fullness we have all received, grace upon grace."

There are two different statements about fullness and completeness in Christ in Colossians 2:9–10. One says Christ is full of everything God is. If we want to encounter God, the fullness of God is there for us to encounter in Christ. There is nowhere else we need to go. The second statement says because we are in Christ, we also have been made full. We have no lack of anything in Him. He gives us everything we really need. Because Christ lacks nothing of the Godhead, we lack nothing in Christ.

Forgiveness is our biggest and ultimate need. As Colossians 2:12–13 says, when we are baptized, we are forgiven by Jesus and through Him. We are made truly and completely full the minute the Spirit touches our foreheads and our hearts in Baptism. We are united with Christ, so every act that we needed to do, He has already done for us. We lack no truth beyond what He has given us because He has given us His Word as well as His Spirit.

πλήρωμα
plērōma: fullness, a filling up.[22]

πεπληρωμένοι
peplērōmenoi: having been made full, complete.[23]

God doesn't forget about the very practical needs of our daily lives though; He continually provides for those as well. Sometimes we don't feel full. Sometimes we lose our job and struggle with a fear of lack; at other times, we struggle with covetousness and discontentment because we compare ourselves to others. God's promise that we are full, no matter the circumstances, is a mystery. It is a mysterious fullness that we have. But it is still a true and real fullness. By now in our study together, we know that when we encounter what is mysterious, we trust what God says, because He knows what is best.

Are there any areas of your life at present where it is hard to see Christ bringing fullness?

How have you seen Him bring this fullness into your life?

There are moments when people's true needs surface, when our deepest need for forgiveness clearly outweighs anything else. In these moments, we remember that the philosophies coming from human wisdom alone are empty, as Paul says in Colossians 2, and that the only true fullness is living forgiven in Christ. Let me tell you a story about one of those moments.

When I was in graduate school for social work, we had many class discussions about helping people find hope. Counseling, at its core, is about instilling hope, helping people believe life can be better than their current situation. One time, a class discussion settled on advocating for women with unplanned pregnancies. After a lengthy conversation regarding the options available to women, I asked the question, "What if a woman comes to you because she is struggling with guilt over a past abortion?"

My professor responded, "I'm not sure that happens."

I politely disagreed: "It happened to me last week when I was working at our local pregnancy center."

My professor opened the conversation to the class. My fellow students suggested listing the good things that had come from the woman's decision or reminding the woman a difficult road had been avoided for both her and the baby. Some students brought up the discussion of whether it was a fetus or a baby that had been aborted. At last, my professor offered the closest thing to wisdom in that discussion: "You tell her she made the best choice she could at the time."

My professor's suggestion wasn't completely offtrack. But her answer was incomplete.

What does the woman who has experienced abortion need?

FORGIVENESS.

What do we need when we lash out at our co-workers, our friends, or our family?

FORGIVENESS.

What do we need when we are undisciplined with our time, our resources, and our abilities?

FORGIVENESS.

We reflect forgiveness when we give grace to one another.

What does the person struggling to find purpose in life need?

MERCY.

What does our friend who is experiencing loss, transition, or change need?

CARE, TENDERNESS, PATIENCE, LOVE.

Any tips we offer about what they should do differently, what has worked for us in the past, or what we think is best should only be offered if they ask, because ultimately, they don't need our human philosophies. What they really need is Jesus and the truth He speaks to them of His complete forgiveness and never-ending love. The only lasting fullness we will ever find is in Him.

The world may offer a lot of philosophies that sound pretty good. Those philosophies may be good, or they may be terrible. Paul reminds us that human wisdom will only get us so far. Fullness is found only in Christ Jesus. It is a fullness we could never think up on our own, we cannot earn, and no one can ever take away.

He fills us mightily. He fills us mysteriously. And we are filled—full, full, and then full some more.

CONNECTED BY THE WORD

Use the Scripture memory verse for the week and the prayer prompt to bring your confession, thanksgiving, praise, and requests before our mighty and mysterious God.

WEEK 3 MEMORY VERSE

In whom are hidden all the treasures of wisdom and knowledge. (Colossians 2:3)

PRAYER PROMPT

Savior, today I need help trusting that I am full and complete in You when lack creeps in . . .

Day 5

THE MYSTERY OF JUDGMENT
COLOSSIANS 2:14–19

"All of this is so nice," you say. "Jesus fills us—yay!" you say. "I'm going to stand in that," you say. But still you have questions:

> How come sometimes we feel full to the brim and sometimes we feel as empty as a flat tire?

> How come the Colossians were still having issues with false teachers?

> How come we still have so many issues in the Church today?

> Shouldn't the Church be the very place we see forgiveness and fullness most clearly?

Those are all great and very honest questions. Our study today will try to address some of them.

Read Colossians 2:14–19 and identify the problem occurring in the Colossian Church.

The Colossians' problem is not foreign to us. Unfortunately, it comes all too easily when we look at one another in the Church.

Notice how one word in Colossians 2:15 and one word in Colossians 2:16 are closely related:

SHAME ⟵⟶ JUDGMENT

Most Scripture translations separate Colossians 2:14–15 from Colossians 2:16–19 with a subheading. That isn't inappropriate, but reading the verses closer together can help us see how the ideas in those verses are connected.

Reread Colossians 2:15–16 below and circle *shame* and *judgment* there:

He disarmed the rulers and authorities and put them to open shame, by triumphing over them in Him. Therefore let no one pass judgment on you in questions of food and drink, or with regard to a festival or a new moon or a Sabbath.
(Colossians 2:15–16)

How would you describe the relationship between shame and judgment?

It's helpful to remember that, biblically speaking, there are two different kinds of judgment:

- God's judgment of man
- Man's judgment of one another

All too often we confuse the two, at least in our subconscious minds. When another human being judges us, it can feel like God is also judging us. And when we judge another person, we often also think that surely God sees them the way we do. And yet that's not the case.

God's judgment, like God Himself, is going to remain somewhat mysterious to us because He is God and we are not. But let's lay some groundwork of what we do know about God's judgment and His grace.

Look through the following Scripture passages and note what stands out to you about the final judgment of mankind.

Matthew 25:31–46

2 Peter 3:4–13

What we know about God's judgment is that Jesus is going to come back for us, and He will judge all people according to His standards of perfection and holiness. The Bible doesn't tell us exactly what all of that will look like. Reading what God's Word does tell us about the final judgment can be scary and shocking. How God's mercy and justice can exist together is part of the mystery. But we trust what God says. And besides telling us that Christ will judge the world when He returns, God's Word also tells us we can be confident what the outcome will be for those who believe in Jesus.

THE VERDICT FOR THOSE WHO TRUST IN CHRIST IS SURE AND CERTAIN GRACE.

THE VERDICT ON OUR LIFE AT THE LAST DAY WILL BE THIS: "CHRIST HAS CANCELED YOUR DEBT."

What promise does Romans 8:1–2 give to you regarding God's judgment?

God's judgment is not a game, characterized by manipulation or surprise rules. As we studied on the second day of week 2, He has revealed to us all we need to know through Jesus and His Word.

Man's judgment is different. It is a game, and we never know if we're winning. This makes man's judgment also mysterious to us—but mysterious in a different way than God's judgment is mysterious. It is mysterious in a painful and frustrating way because the rules keep changing, depending on whom we're talking to at the time.

Man's judgment caused the problems in Colossae that Paul was writing about, and it causes countless problems for Christians today too. It causes problems because it wasn't supposed to be part of life in the first place.

Read Colossians 2:16–19 again below. Underline any word or phrase that describes the kind of judgment the false teachers in the Church at Colossae were placing on the Colossian believers.

Therefore, let no one pass judgment on you in questions of food and drink, or with regard to a festival or a new moon or a Sabbath. These are a shadow of the things to come, but the substance belongs to Christ. Let no one disqualify you, insisting on asceticism and worship of angels, going on in detail about visions, puffed up without reason by his sensuous mind, and not holding fast to the Head, from whom the whole body, nourished and knit together through its joints and ligaments, grows with a growth that is from God. (Colossians 2:16–19)

How do Christian believers purposefully or inadvertently try to disqualify one another in the Christian walk of life? In your own context specifically, what do you hear people insisting on for others?

How does this disqualifying and insisting create shame among the followers of Jesus?

Paul says, "Let no one pass judgment on you." Why should this disqualifying and shaming be absent from Christian communities, according to Colossians 2:14–19?

When Christ died on the cross, the devil thought he won. There was probably a party and celebrating. It's like that moment in the superhero movie where the villain's smile slowly spreads, confident that he has won . . . but then the superhero shows up and there's no way the villain stands a chance. Satan did not see Jesus' Easter victory coming. Just like in a superhero film, the end when the villain tucks tail and runs is the sweetest.

The description of Christ's victory in Colossians 2:14–15 is one of my favorites. Jesus canceled our debt. And not only did He disarm the rulers and authorities, but He completely put them to shame when He died and rose again.

The Greek word for "shame" in Colossians 2:15 is related to exposure. Shame lays bare all someone has done, the heart of who they are, striking at our identity hard. Using shame, Satan tries to declare, "Look at you! Look what you've done, the disaster you make of things. You are not worthy." But Paul in these verses says Jesus' victory turned shame on its head.

δειγματίζω
deigmatizō: to expose, make a show of[24]

GOD HAS A PURPOSE FOR SHAME AND IT'S NOT YOU AND ME.

Jesus' death and resurrection took away our shame and turned the shame instead onto Satan and his evil spirits, because of all they have done to destroy the people and creation that belong to God.

Because of Jesus, Christians now have a different relationship with shame.

SHAME HAS BEEN OVERCOME.

Jesus paid for all of our mess. He wiped our hearts, our minds, and our hands clean, and He continues to do so constantly. Therefore, shame has no place in our relationship with God, our relationships with others, or our relationship with ourselves.

It is appropriate for God's people to experience guilt when we sin. But there's an important difference between guilt and shame.

Shame sits in us and tries to separate us from God.

Guilt turns us to Christ, and He pours forgiveness into us.

Only Jesus gets to say who we are now:

children of God (1 John 3:1)

full of life (John 10:10)

friend of God (John 15:14–15)

advocated for (Romans 8:34)

free (Galatians 5:1)

How does Christ's victory over all shame address what people would insist on for our lives today?

There will always be people who want to insist on things other than Christ and who try to disqualify others based on those things. Those people harped on the Colossians, and they'll harp on us too. As the Church, we stand together against the temptation to be sucked into judging one another by these disqualifiers.

Look at Colossians 2:18–19 again. How do we as Christians together respond to insistences, disqualifications, and details that do not come from God's Word?

We're going to hold fast, and we're going to do it together.

What does the act of holding fast to Christ look like? Paul used the analogy of a body holding fast to a head. What does that analogy indicate about the connection between Christ and us in the Church? Can you think of some examples of times when you held fast to Christ with other believers or as a whole congregation of believers?

Doing life together and doing it well is not an easy task. Even when we know that Christ completely took away all of the shame of every one of us, our natural inclination is still to judge one another. That's why Paul kept pointing the Colossians back to what Christ has done. It's easy for "Jesus died for you" to become a rote message. But as we hear over and over again what Christ has done, the Holy Spirit changes our hearts and minds so that we hold fast to Christ together instead of judging one another. On our mysterious walk with Christ (day 3 of this week), God is the one who gives the growth and nourishment we need so that we are Christ's knit-together Body—not separated by judgment and shame, but so closely connected to one another and to Him.

Holding fast is a good visual. We hold fast to one another, grabbing our fellow Christians by the shirtsleeve so that neither we nor they get blown away by the winds of change or deception around us. Together we hold fast to the Word and the gifts God gives us in His Church because that's where He has promised to be. We hold fast and let Him be the Head—this mighty and mysterious Jesus.

CONNECTED BY THE WORD

Use the Scripture memory verse for the week and the prayer prompt to bring your confession, thanksgiving, praise, and requests before our mighty and mysterious God.

WEEK 3 MEMORY VERSE

In whom are hidden all the treasures of wisdom and knowledge. (Colossians 2:3)

PRAYER PROMPT

Savior, take away any shame the devil would try to throw at me. Forgive me, renew me in Your grace and hope. Help me to hold fast to You with others, rather than disqualifying or judging my brothers and sisters . . .

The Place of Words in Connection

God is a God of words. He spoke, and the universe was created. His prophets spoke, and what they said happened and was true. Jesus spoke a word, and a little girl was raised from the dead, a woman's blood flow was stopped, a blind man could see, and a lame man could walk. And God gave us His written Word so that we could trust His plans and promises for the salvation of the whole world. According to John 1, Jesus *is* the Word. The Word made flesh.

WE DIDN'T CREATE COMMUNICATION AND CONNECTION.

GOD DID.

God connects with us now via His Word. Even when He connects with us through His body and blood in bread and wine at the table of His altar and when He connects with us by washing us with water, His Word is what gives those things power.

God also tells us to speak His Word and words that reflect Him to one another—whether in our families or among our local congregation and community of believers.

How many words do you speak in a day? How many of them purposefully connect you to God or to others? How many speak life? Sometimes it's a challenge to know what speaks life and hope and what speaks judgment.

Here's a small list of words that I have noticed speak judgment:

- That's not the way I would do it.
- Don't they know better?
- What were they thinking?
- How can they even?
- I'm not your typical . . .
- Raising 'em right!

Here's a small list of words that I have noticed speak Jesus' life and hope and connection to people around us, rather than judgment:

- Tell me more.
- Help me understand.
- I'm glad you're here.
- What do you need?
- How can I help?
- I noticed.
- You are loved.
- Jesus changes everything.

JOHN 1:14

"And the Word became flesh and dwelt among us, and we have seen His glory, glory as of the only Son from the Father, full of grace and truth."

ROMANS 8:16

"The Spirit Himself testifies with our spirit that we are God's children." (NIV)

COLOSSIANS 3:16

"Let the word of Christ dwell in you richly, teaching and admonishing one another in all wisdom, singing psalms and hymns and spiritual songs, with thankfulness in your hearts to God."

DEUTERONOMY 6:6–9

"These commandments that I give you today are to be on your hearts. Impress them on your children. Talk about them when you sit at home and when you walk along the road, when you lie down and when you get up. Tie them as symbols on your hands and bind them on your foreheads. Write them on the doorframes of your houses and on your gates." (NIV)

Week 4

ALL THAT IS MESSIANIC

Viewer Guide

VIDEO 4: THE GOOD LIFE* AND THE BEST LIFE
COLOSSIANS 2:20–3:1

Colossians was an encyclical letter—a letter written to be shared in more than one location.**

Paul tells them the best life can only be found in Jesus Christ.

SEE COLOSSIANS 2:20–3:1.

PAUL'S WARNINGS

1. Beware of systems that help us _____ _____

_____.

SEE COLOSSIANS 2:20–22.

IF WITH CHRIST

---

*   See Trip Lee, *The Good Life* (Chicago, IL: Moody Publishers, 2012).

**   *Lutheran Bible Companion*, vol. 2 (St. Louis, MO: Concordia Publishing House, 2014), 526, 555.

Do not let someone make a *must* of what God calls a *maybe*.

2. Beware of the "good life" defined as the life that _____ _____

_____—or _____ _____.

SEE COLOSSIANS 2:23.

> *Good* as God defines it is almost always different from how the world defines it.

3. Beware of anything that presents someone as "_____

_____."

SEE COLOSSIANS 3:1.

> Our response: "I have been raised *with Christ*."

PSALM 91:2 (NLT)

This I declare about the LORD: He alone is my refuge, my place of safety; he is my God, and I trust him.

DISCUSSION QUESTIONS

1. What systems, ideas, or teachings have been helpful in your life? How do we prevent those things from taking the place of Jesus Christ in our hearts and lives?

2. What "do not" or "don't touch" commands are common in the Christian Church today? How can we walk with Jesus in a way that is a good witness, without also making regulations more important than faith in Jesus?

3. Look at James 1:17. Now look at all of James 1. What can we learn in this chapter about how God defines *good*? What other Scripture passages come to mind as you consider what God calls good in this life?

Day 1

DYING TO A THOUSAND THINGS
COLOSSIANS 2:16–23

One benefit to having a work-from-home kind of gig is my ability to go on fourth-grade field trips. Fourth grade is one of the best grades for field trips. At that age, kids' ability to read chapter books, their longer attention spans, and the childhood curiosity they still possess means really cool field trips that even adults can't resist.

This last autumn, I hopped on a bus with sixty or so fourth graders for the field trip of the century. Yes, you guessed it . . . we went to the University of Nebraska at Lincoln, home of the one, the only, the Cornhuskers. It was fun, and while everyone else was there for the stadium tour, I was really there for the Museum of Natural History. Woolly mammoths win out any day over football at our house. (Shhhh . . . don't tell anyone in Nebraska I said that.)

Spending my day hanging with a crew of delightful fourth-grade girls giggling over the bones of giant sloths filled my happiness tank for a month. My favorite portion of the visit was when we walked through the "Hall of Evolution." Maybe that wasn't the exact name of the room, but that was the gimmick of it—a walkthrough of interactive exhibits presenting the evolution of DNA and other genetic and microbiological concepts in a way even children could understand. It was a fun room, and the girls were engrossed in flipping up displays, turning spinning devices, and peeking in little windows. I couldn't help but take issue with the room, though, for this reason: theories were being presented as facts, and scientific possibilities were being presented as absolutes. As the girls and I walked out of the room, I asked them,

EVOLUTION
The belief that all that exists developed and diversified over time through a very slow process of simpler microorganisms and cells becoming more complex beings.

"You guys know we believe very little of all that, right?"

One little towhead cutie looked me in the eye and eloquently said, "Well, yeah [insert unspoken "duh"]. It's like we can read Percy Jackson and not believe in it!"

Exactly.

In this life, we take all kinds of ideas, theories, beliefs, and information into our brains. As we talked about in Video 3, fusion is a tempting but not necessarily right response. As we encounter all that is around us, we need to constantly be asking ourselves, "Do I believe this? What are the implications of this idea?" and even more important, we ask, "What does God say about this?"

My fourth-grade field trip fellow adventurers reminded me that some of the things we take in have the *appearance of wisdom*—just as Paul said in Colossians 2:23. In a short span of verses, Paul contrasts the things having an appearance of wisdom with what is true wisdom—that which gives hope.

What, according to Colossians 2:20, is the mechanism that changes our lives from hopeless to hopeful, from the appearance of wisdom to true wisdom?

COLOSSIANS 2:23
"These have indeed an appearance of wisdom in promoting self-made religion and asceticism and severity to the body, but they are of no value in stopping the indulgence of the flesh."

But if Colossians 2:20 is about change happening in our lives, why on earth does Paul specifically say, "If with Christ you *died*"? Well, there's an important parallel introductory statement in 3:1. Can you find it?

It turns out that the Holy Spirit through Paul's letters says a lot about dying and rising to new life with Christ. How do the following verses add to your understanding of the significance of dying and rising with Christ?

Romans 6:3–5

Galatians 2:20

2 Timothy 2:11

1 CORINTHIANS 15:54–57
"When the perishable puts on the imperishable, and the mortal puts on immortality, then shall come to pass the saying that is written: 'Death is swallowed up in victory.' 'O death, where is your victory? O death, where is your sting?' The sting of death is sin, and the power of sin is the law. But thanks be to God, who gives us the victory through our Lord Jesus Christ."

Dying sounds like such a terrible thing—and it is. There is nothing natural about death. God intended for us to live, not die. But sin brought death into the world, and death now affects all of us because we all are steeped in sin. There is no escaping it. And yet God takes even the thing that is the consequence of our rebellion against Him and He redeems it. Christ died on the cross so that we might not die eternally. Because He rose from the dead, His death took the sting out of death. As mind-bending as it sounds, when we are baptized, we become part of Christ's death, and therefore our physical death one day doesn't hold the same burden, the same sting. Dying with Christ in our Baptism is the only dying that isn't futile. Instead, dying with Christ opens a whole new life afterward—a life in Him. And anything with Christ is far from futile.

The Colossians were very confused. They had died with Christ in Baptism and been raised to new life in Him. But the false teachers they were listening to were saying, "Yeah, that's nice, but you still need . . ."

Look at Colossians 2:20–3:1 below, and circle words or phrases that indicate what the false teachers wanted the Colossians to do or attain:

> If with Christ you died to the elemental spirits of the world, why, as if you were still alive in the world, do you submit to regulations—"Do not handle, Do not taste, Do not touch" (referring to things that all perish as they are used)—according to human precepts and teachings? These have indeed an appearance of wisdom in promoting self-made religion and asceticism and severity to the body, but they are of no value in stopping the indulgence of the flesh. If then you have been raised with Christ, seek the things that are above, where Christ is, seated at the right hand of God. (Colossians 2:20–3:1)

ASCETICISM
The harsh discipline of the body for religious reasons, such as the avoidance of foods, beating the body, or other ways to deny the flesh in order to prove rejection of the things of the world and prioritization of the things of God. Asceticism is often also coupled with false humility.

Our sinful nature naturally prefers self-made religion. Because it means we are in control—and it operates on a system that makes sense to us: "Do the things that are right, and don't do the things that are wrong." It seems so much easier. But Christianity is not about rules. Religion made by the one true God is about only one thing: being in Christ.

This is why the First Commandment is the foundation that undergirds every other command from God.

DEUTERONOMY 5:6–7
"I am the LORD your God, who brought you out of the land of Egypt, out of the house of slavery. 'You shall have no other gods before Me.'"

Read Deuteronomy 6:4–5. What connection can you see between these verses and the First Commandment in Deuteronomy 5:6–7? (Hint: See Matthew 22:36–40 for Jesus' words on the matter.)

Colossians and these Deuteronomy texts proclaim the same message:

CHRIST IS ALL.

Therefore, we die to everything else but the one true God—the triune God. For the Colossians, it was regulations of ritual and a pantheon of spirits to worship. These may be an issue for us, but often ideas are what vie for our attention. There are thousands of things that try to say they are as important as Christ. They may not be inherently bad things. But they become a problem when we let them take the place of Christ or share His throne. So we die to them in Christ. And that gives us power to say to them, "I don't need you." We can visit the museums, watch the documentaries, listen attentively to our friends who have ideas that don't align with Christ, and yet walk away, still secure in Christ, saying to ideas that don't mesh with His Word, "I don't need you."

When you look at the list Paul gives in Colossians 2:16–23, what connections do you see to the things swirling around you?

Here are some modern counterparts to the elemental spirits, festivals, new moons, angel worship, and human teachings that come to my mind:

> **Witchcraft**—The Bible is clear we are not supposed to toy with witchcraft of any kind. It leads down a dark road very quickly. Have you noticed, though, that darkness can be trendy? Occasionally our culture vacillates toward treating darkness and different expressions of witchcraft as cool or vogue.

Can you give any examples of dark arts being glorified or made light of in our culture?

> **Magic**—There are all kinds of expressions of magic in our entertainment: in the books we read, the games we play, and the movies we watch. Sometimes it's harmless and even useful for teaching, like C. S. Lewis's Chronicles of Narnia series. Sometimes we can start to think of it as having power to affect our lives in ways that, in actuality, only God can and should. But we can't take it all in without ever asking questions or discerning things. Perhaps this warning against magic seems unnecessary to you, since so much

THE MESSIAH
When we say that Jesus is the *Messiah*, we use a Hebrew title from the Old Testament that became the Greek title *Christ* in the New Testament. The people at the time of the New Testament were expecting a Messiah—someone anointed by God to save His people—but they were not expecting the Messiah to be who Jesus is: God's Son, the Second Person of the Trinity. Today when we call Jesus *Messiah*, we mean that He is the one who saves us, the one who reveals God to us, and the one who is the only intermediary we need between God the Father and us.

מָשִׁיחַ
Messiah (Hebrew)

Χριστός
Christ (Greek)

"He found first his own brother Simon and said to him, 'We have found the Messiah' (which translated means Christ)." (John 1:41, NASB)

AUTHOR'S NOTE
For some biblical warnings against witchcraft, magic, mediums, and dark arts, see the following passages:

1 Chronicles 10:13–14

Leviticus 19:31

Galatians 5:19–21

Revelation 21:8

of the magic in our culture is meant for entertainment. I personally do read a very diverse range of books and watch lots of different movies. But have you ever seen an instance in which someone took "entertainment" magic a little too seriously?

> When we pick up a book, a movie, or a game, it's good to ask ourselves, "Am I a person who can read this and not *believe* in it? Is my child a person who can read this and not *believe* in it?"

> And from time to time, it is good to ask ourselves as an individual or as a family, "Do I/we need tighter boundaries? What boundaries might I/we need in order to help us discern what is good for entertainment versus what goes too far?"

Mother Nature—Stewardship of creation is important—very important. We were given the beautiful gift of God's creation all around us. It's a problem, though, when people start talking about God's creation as a separate, spiritual being, such as when people try to connect with or honor "Mother Earth." When we respect and care for the environment, let's point to the God who created it.

Astrology and horoscopes—God created the stars. He knows each one by name. He set them in place to mark seasons and to give light. When we find hidden meaning in them, when we trust them, even in silly ways like horoscopes, we are putting something in the place where only God should be in our lives.

Evolutionary thought—We've already talked in our study about some of the problems with evolution, according to a Christian perspective. Here, I will only say that all too often we trust science more than we trust God. God's Word testifies that God created the world and that He performs miracles. Since He created all things, He also created science. Science is a gift to us when it helps us learn about God's world and helps us praise Him for what He has made. But science is not a gift used rightly when it is used to raise doubt about God's Word. We hold to God's Word as our foundation, and from there we try to learn about God's world with our tools and books and hypotheses.

Fascination with angels—It's easy to give angels a much too special, almost godlike space in our lives. We don't pray to angels. No one becomes an angel when they die. Hebrews 1:3–4 reminds us that the angels are lower than Jesus, not alongside Jesus. Christ came to earth as man, subjecting Himself "for a little while" to humility as one of us. That little while ended when He burst forth triumphant from the grave. The angels sing Christ's praise in His presence. The angels bow to Him. And we do too. Christ is whom we worship.

AUTHOR'S NOTE

Let me be clear: Ouija boards or games that directly invoke ghosts or spirits—not cool, ever. Always dangerous and forbidden. Please see the Bible verses that address dark arts in the previous author's note for more on this.

Which things from the list above do you see most often in our culture today?

What Paul says happened to us "with Christ" is better than any pseudospirit, pseudolight, or pseudohope this world could offer us. Dying with Christ means dying to everything that is not of Christ. It is like dying a thousand deaths every day; but the result is the very best and it's always the same: true life, true light, true hope in Christ alone. As we die to a thousand things, He gives us resurrection joy, allowing us to come face-to-face with what is not of Him and say, "While that is interesting, I don't believe in *that*. I believe in *Him*."

CONNECTED BY THE WORD

Use the Scripture memory verse for the week and the prayer prompt to bring your confession, thanksgiving, praise, and requests before our mighty and mysterious God.

WEEK 4 MEMORY VERSE

When Christ who is your life appears, then you also will appear with Him in glory. (Colossians 3:4)

PRAYER PROMPT

Jesus, help me to see You as the center of my life. Help me die to all that would seek to take a place beside You, alongside You, or instead of You, such as . . .

Day 2

SPIRITUAL WARFARE CLEANUP
COLOSSIANS 2:20–23

When I was in seventh grade, a friend came over to my house on a non-descript Friday. As we were sitting on my bed giggling about what boys we liked, she pulled out a deck of tarot cards. She told me it would be fun to lay out some of the cards and see what they said about boys and about our future lives. I was game because my seventh-grade self—much like my thirty-eight-year-old self—jumped into any situation four hundred times too quickly without ever thinking. My mom walked into my bedroom to ask about snacks or some other mundane thing and quietly lost her stuff. It was the look of intensity in her eyes that said, "I mean business," when her words simply said, "Girls, put those away and come sit in the kitchen."

I prepped for a lecture of supreme embarrassment, and that is exactly what I got. The embarrassment wore away eventually. What I remember more is one sentence my mom said that day that was more meaningful to me than anything else she could have said on darkness and light, trust and God's plans:

"I HAVE KNOWN DARKNESS, AND I DON'T WANT IT TO HAVE ANY PART OF YOU."

I never messed with tarot cards again. My mom's response got my attention. My parents were generally pretty flexible in the realm of adolescent parenting. They didn't have a lot of rules, but when they did have rules, you listened.

As I grew up, I started to notice that darkness wasn't always so obvious, and that even things that were bad for me were hard to give up.

SOMETIMES LIFE IS SLUSHY.

Read Colossians 2:20–23 in the three different translations below. Note the differences in each translation that help you understand the verses better:

NIV	NASB	NLT
Since you died with Christ to the elemental spiritual forces of this world, why, as though you still belonged to the world, do you submit to its rules: "Do not handle! Do not taste! Do not touch!"? These rules, which have to do with things that are all destined to perish with use, are based on merely human commands and teachings. Such regulations indeed have an appearance of wisdom, with their self-imposed worship, their false humility and their harsh treatment of the body, but they lack any value in restraining sensual indulgence.	If you have died with Christ to the elementary principles of the world, why, as if you were living in the world, do you submit yourself to decrees, such as, "Do not handle, do not taste, do not touch!" (which all refer to things destined to perish with use)—in accordance with the commandments and teachings of men? These are matters which have, to be sure, the appearance of wisdom in self-made religion and self-abasement and severe treatment of the body, but are of no value against fleshly indulgence.	You have died with Christ, and he has set you free from the spiritual powers of this world. So why do you keep on following the rules of the world, such as, "Don't handle! Don't taste! Don't touch!"? Such rules are mere human teachings about things that deteriorate as we use them. These rules may seem wise because they require strong devotion, pious self-denial, and severe bodily discipline. But they provide no help in conquering a person's evil desires.

They can be called "forces," "principles," or "powers," but all of these words remind us that there is a far larger scheme going on all around us. Paul expands on the war against spiritual darkness in Ephesians 6.

Read Ephesians 6:10–12. What descriptors of the darkness do you find in these verses?

Spiritual warfare can be disconcerting. The reality of darkness is not something to take lightly. But it's also helpful to remember that Jesus has already won the war. We are now in war cleanup. That's why it feels so muddy and murky—slushy, if you will. Darkness still manifests itself, and we still encounter it. But trying to identify when and where it occurs is not easy. This present darkness is powerful, but it isn't the war. It brings to my mind stories and pictures from the days and months after V-E Day in World War II. The war had ended, but Europe was still a mess.

THE WAR AGAINST DARKNESS HAS BEEN WON. BUT THAT DOESN'T MAKE THE CLEANUP ANY LESS MESSY.

No one likes the casualties of war. Often, even as Christians, we would much rather hold onto the things Christ calls us to die to. It can be much more appealing to coexist with something that is not of Jesus than to rip it away.

Darkness doesn't usually stand up and announce itself either. Sometimes things are all the more destructive and dangerous because they seem so palatable. The New Living Translation of Colossians 2:20 above specifically mentions the darkness of spiritual powers in this spiritual warfare cleanup. But power among and between people is another source of darkness that is often unclear. Power, in some ways, is a necessary part of life to prevent all-out anarchy. Yet human power can be used by Satan in very spiritually evil and dark ways.

Where do you see power at work in the world for good?

Where do you see power at work in the world for destruction or outright evil?

In what ways do the lines blur between the good and the evil that power produces? Can you think of some examples of when power appeared to be a good thing at the beginning but then took an unexpected turn and became destructive?

Perhaps an extreme example is Hitler's rise to power in Germany in the 1930s. Some people were concerned from the beginning about Hitler's ideology and how he might act on it when he received political power. But Hitler didn't stand up and declare himself as darkness. What he offered sounded like hope and seemed to be light at first. For many people, the evils and atrocities eventually caused by Hitler's power were a shock.

Even in less extreme scenarios, rarely do we see darkness coming straight at us. Sometimes we become involved in something that seems to be light, or that at least seems neutral, and then eventually we realize it is darkness or has turned toward darkness—but it can be hard to recognize this before the darkness has already done some, if not much, damage. To complicate the matter, God designed us to be connected to one another in relationships, and yet our relationships are probably one of the most frequent places unexpected assaults from darkness come at us. We find ourselves in a relationship that we think is good for us, full of light. Then unexpectedly, we realize the relationship has become unhealthy, and there is darkness in it before we realize it. At that point, separating ourselves from that relationship or setting up significant boundaries so that it cannot bring darkness into our lives is important, though often very painful.

The Colossians found themselves in such a position with the false teachers among them. They had walked into things of darkness without realizing it. When Paul wrote to them, they needed to double back and set boundaries in those relationships in order to not become completely confused and shrouded in the darkness. Their experience testifies that the Church is not immune from unwittingly walking into darkness, just as individuals are not immune from walking into darkness.

How has the Church on earth responded well when darkness has been uncovered in her midst?

How has the Church on earth not responded well when darkness has been uncovered in her midst?

One of the most painful ways power has been abused systemically in the United States and has been used by Satan to spread darkness—inside and outside the church—is through disparate treatment of and discrimination (whether active or passive) toward people according to their race. In the book *I'm Still Here: Black Dignity in a World Made for Whiteness*, Austin Channing Brown bravely and boldly implores the church to allow for an open and ongoing conversation about this darkness. We may think this darkness doesn't exist anymore, especially in the church. But Channing Brown asks us in the church to stare this darkness in the face rather than pretend it doesn't exist. As she does so, she also beautifully points to the only true hope in the midst of any darkness:

> It's haunting. But it's also holy. And when we talk about race today, with all the pain packed into the conversation, the Holy Spirit remains in the room.[13]

The Holy Spirit is the hope in our midst, whether the darkness we confront in our own lives, in our communities, and in our churches is racism, ethnocentricism, human trafficking, sexual abuse, dishonest use of money, addiction, working too much, working too little, or anything else. There is pain wrapped up with things of darkness. But the Holy Spirit remains in the room and does not leave us as we work through the darkness, as we address it, as we confront it—together.

Paul says the same thing to the Colossians as they figure out how to confront the darkness of the false teaching among them: the Holy Spirit remains in the room.

What do John 14:16 and 14:26 tell us about what the Holy Spirit does in the midst of the spiritual warfare cleanup?

Living in the messiness—the slush—of spiritual warfare cleanup is not easy. But the Holy Spirit helps, advocates, and comforts through the dark and difficult conversations. The Holy Spirit's power does change lives, churches, communities. The darkness will continue to try to creep in, but we have a Helper, and that makes all the difference. Christ has overcome, once and for all. And He is in us. Jesus has known darkness and has defeated the darkness; so, while it may push against us and try to find a place in our lives, it can have no part of us. Praise God for His mighty help in the aftermath of the war He has won.

CONNECTED BY THE WORD

Use the Scripture memory verse for the week and the prayer prompt to bring your confession, thanksgiving, praise, and requests before our mighty and mysterious God.

WEEK 4 MEMORY VERSE

When Christ who is your life appears, then you also will appear with Him in glory. (Colossians 3:4)

PRAYER PROMPT

Jesus, You rescue us from darkness in the spiritual warfare cleanup. Help us to live in Your victory over darkness; help us to have hard conversations and confront darkness of all kinds because You promise the Holy Spirit is with us as we do so . . .

Day 3

HIDDEN WITH CHRIST
COLOSSIANS 3:1–4

How often do you come face-to-face with the mightiness of God? When do you find yourself thinking about God's mightiness the most?

We tend to think about God's mightiness and power primarily when we consider creation or miracles. Less often do we consider how God revealing Himself through the Messiah, Jesus Christ, is an amazing act of God's mightiness and power. Our text today points us directly to the work of Jesus as the Messiah as a reflection of the mightiness of God. Our text today shows us that, though Jesus did many miracles during His time on earth (healing many people, walking on water, feeding thousands with just a few loaves of bread and a few fish), the greatest work showing His might was His death and resurrection, giving us Life—Life with a capital *L*.

If you asked a random person on the street to define the word *life*, what do you think he or she would say?

Now read Colossians 3:1–4 and define the word *life* according to these verses.

Life can be full of wonderful things, and life can be hard. Yet Paul says to the Colossians that life is no life without Christ. We breathe, eat salad (or steak), play at the park, go for a run, drive to school, return an email at work, but Paul says it's only really *life*—true life, the way God intended it to be—when we're connected to Jesus.

In John 10:10, Jesus talks about the life He has come to bring.

Write out John 10:10 in the space below and circle Jesus' description of the mighty and mysterious life He offers us.

So many mighty things are wrapped up in that one little word *life*! Colossians 3:1–4 reveals to us three components of this abundant Life. We can also describe it as the mighty Life found in a mighty Messiah. When we share in the Messiah's mighty Life, our everyday existence may still look ordinary, but it has, in fact, become extraordinary because our lives have become part of the Messiah making Himself known to the world through us.

THREE COMPONENTS OF OUR MIGHTY LIFE HIDDEN IN A MIGHTY MESSIAH

1. The Power of Pilgrimage

We live in a paradox in this abundant Life in Christ. Colossians 3:2 confirms the pull we feel in opposite directions:

> Set your minds on things that are above, not on things that are on earth. (Colossians 3:2)

It's like we are supposed to have one foot here on earth and also both feet firmly planted near Christ's throne in heaven. It seems impossible. But Paul gives the reason why we're supposed to set our minds above and have two feet there while one is still on earth:

> For you have died, and your life is hidden with Christ in God. (Colossians 3:3)

There's the idea of dying with Christ again. We saw this before in Colossians 2:12, as well as in 2:20. Our life apart from Jesus ended at our Baptism. Ever since, our life has been wrapped up with and in His.

Because we are connected to Christ, our daily lives are important, but what is more important is the big story that our lives have become a part of. Our daily lives are now part of the pilgrimage: Life with Jesus. Life with Jesus has begun now, in the midst of our daily lives, but it will go on forever, even after our daily lives on earth have ended.

This greatly impacts how we define life and Life. Though it's good to seek good things during this life, such as having enough of what we need to eat and live and thrive and having meaningful work and a way to provide for our families, in the end, provision and security are only found in Christ. Some days it feels like Christ and a perfect, tear-free eternity with Him are far away. Colossians tells us this is because our Life with Christ is hidden—not fully visible or understood—until the day He returns.

Fill in the missing pieces of Colossians 3:3–4 below, and reflect on how powerful this truth is for us in our pilgrimage on this earth:

For you have died, and your life is hidden with Christ in God. When _____ _____ _____ _____ _____ appears, then you also will appear with Him in glory.

Being disconnected from Christ, even a little bit, is like being disconnected from a part of ourselves. Christ Himself *is* our Life—and yet He's hidden from our sight for now. That's the challenge of the pilgrimage. But in the meantime, He continues to give us Himself—our very Life—in the mysterious work of these things: Baptism, the Lord's Supper, and His Word. And because He connects us to Himself over and over through these things, we are reminded that we are going somewhere on this pilgrimage. This journey isn't aimless or futile.

2. The Power of Providence
What phrase do you see repeated in Colossians 3:1–2? In relation to that repeated phrase, what two actions are we told to take?

Christ connects us to the "things that are above" even as He cares for us in the midst of the "things that are on earth." God creates, sustains, and provides for us in a multitude of ways. The life we have even now in this one-foot-on-earth, two-feet-in-heaven pilgrimage is abundant because it is Christ's own Life that He gives us and brings us into. Some of the ways we see His providence are the food on our tables, people in our families, and hope in our lives because of the salvation He gives. At other times, we "seek the things that are above," but it can be very tricky to see how the "things that are above" help with the problems in our life on earth. It can be very hard to see God's providence at times like that.

Often it is when we are lacking reconciliation in our relationships that we strongly feel our need for God's providence. It can be especially frustrating when we long for God's mercy, grace, and forgiveness to work in our relationships but it doesn't seem to be happening.

A story that often encourages me as I look for God's providence in my relationships is how God brought reconciliation to Joseph and his brothers. Joseph's family situation was one of the messiest we ever hear about in Scripture, but God did not give up on any of them. God was in it for the long haul. And though it took many years, eventually the relationship between Joseph and his brothers healed.

Read Genesis 45:1–15. Summarize how God's providence is evident in these verses.

Sometimes, no matter how much we pray about something and "seek the things that are above" concerning it, we will not see how God is working in it until Christ who is our Life appears. But we trust Him concerning even the things that make no sense in our lives, since He is the one sitting at the right hand of God. And one day we will be with Him forever and will get to see His providence perfectly and in fullness forever.

3. The Power of Glory and Grace

Paul says that because our true life is hidden with Christ during our pilgrimage, when Christ appears then our true life will appear with Him also—in glory. *Glory* is kind of a cryptic word. In Colossians 3:4, "glory" is talking about something we don't see yet. The only other time this word shows up in Colossians is in 1:27. There, "glory" is used once to describe something we *do* see now—the mystery (which is Christ) revealed—and once to describe something we don't see yet ("the hope of glory"). When we talked about Jesus being the "image of all" on day 2 of week 2, we talked about Moses asking to see God's glory in Exodus 33:18. The glory that we do not yet see is the same glory God did not allow Moses to see.

What is crazy, though, is that here in Colossians 3:4, Paul is saying we are going to share in that same glory. It is the glory Jesus has with His Father, and we're going to get to share in it. That is an incredible promise!

But God has not left us alone to grasp after His glory while we wait for that day when we will fully see Jesus' glory and share in it. Instead, He gives us glimpses of His glory. Those glimpses are also the ways He promises to give us His grace till He comes back—through His Word, through Baptism, and through Jesus' Supper.

COLOSSIANS 1:27
"To them God chose to make known how great among the Gentiles are the riches of the glory of this mystery, which is Christ in you, the hope of glory."

JOHN 17:5, 22
Jesus prayed on the night of His Last Supper with His disciples:

"And now, Father, glorify Me in Your own presence with the glory that I had with You before the world existed. . . . The glory that You have given Me I have given to them, that they may be one even as We are one."

Look at John 1:14, 16–18. Describe the relationship between God's grace and God's glory according to these verses.

The bottom line is that our Life is hidden with Christ. We may not see clearly where our pilgrimage is going in the near future. We may not understand how He is providing for us in our day-to-day lives. The day when we will be glorified with Him may seem very far away. But the mighty Life we have in our mighty Messiah is ours even now, and He will sustain us till He appears again.

In Luke 14:16–24, Jesus tells a parable about God inviting people to His banquet, inviting them to share in this mighty Life of the mighty Messiah. In the book *Love Does*, author Bob Goff reflects on this incredible invitation:

> I think every day God sends us an invitation to live and sometimes we forget to show up or get head-faked into thinking we haven't really been invited. But you see, we have been invited—every day, all over again.
>
> There's no doubt Jesus invites us to have some very cool experiences in our lives, and for that matter, in the afterlife. Jesus tells a story in the Bible about a rich guy who had a banquet. The rich guy invited lots of people, but most of them made excuses and didn't come, so the guy sent his servants to invite other folks—but this time he invited the unlikely ones, people who normally don't get invited to anything, folks like me. The message he had for this new round of people was simple: "There's more room." That was it. . . . I think God sends out His messengers to tell everybody there's plenty of room and there's free food and conversation and adventure and a wonderful and generous host who has invited us by name. . . . Jesus wants us to come. . . . The one who has invited you is way more powerful than any of the impediments we think we're facing, and He has just one message for us. He leans forward and whispers quietly to each of us, "There's more room."[14]

Christ tells us time and time again that God wants to do life with us. He does not remain in His lofty clouds, tapping on His Apple Watch, mindlessly filling time, ignoring us. Our Life is hidden with Him. But even while it is hidden, we fully belong to Him right now. And He comes among us even now—through His Word, through other Christians, and through His gifts of grace—as we wait to see our Life fully made known.

It's mysterious, it's mighty, and it's messianic—this beautiful, hidden, gracious, glorious, abundant Life.

ISAIAH 25:6–8

"On this mountain the LORD of hosts will make for all peoples

a feast of rich food, a feast of well-aged wine,

of rich food full of marrow, of aged wine well refined.

And He will swallow up on this mountain

the covering that is cast over all peoples,

the veil that is spread over all nations.

He will swallow up death forever;

and the Lord GOD will wipe away tears from all faces,

and the reproach of His people He will take away from all the earth,

for the LORD has spoken."

Connected by the Word

Use the Scripture memory verse for the week and the prayer prompt to bring your confession, thanksgiving, praise, and requests before our mighty and mysterious God.

Week 4 Memory Verse

When Christ who is your life appears, then you also will appear with Him in glory. (Colossians 3:4)

Prayer Prompt

Jesus Christ, my Life is hidden in You. Because You are mighty and mysterious, my Life in You is also mighty and mysterious. That comforts me today because . . .

Day 4

SEEKING & SETTING ON A SAVIOR
COLOSSIANS 3:1–4

"Scripture is like an onion" is one of my new favorite phrases. I find this onion analogy useful for the times when we look at a verse and have a hard time finding Jesus or His grace in it. In those moments, it's helpful to remember that a single Scripture verse is part of God's Word as a whole. The central message of God's Word as a whole is that Jesus is the Savior. Therefore, the message of Christ as Savior is at the center—the center of the onion—for every verse in Scripture. The layers of the onion—the various applications and insights from the Scripture verse for our faith in Christ and for our lives—become clear to us through the work of the Holy Spirit. The Holy Spirit shows us these layers of a Scripture verse or passage through things like spending time noticing the connections between Scripture passages, discussing God's Word with other Christians, and hearing accounts of God's Word working in people's lives. There are never-ending applications and insights that God's Word provides for our lives, while Jesus as Savior at the core remains always the same.

The endless possible layers of the onion are also the reason why we have sometimes spent two to three days in our study on the same verses in Colossians rather than moving briskly through them!

Let's practice our onion-peeling skills on one of the most well-known verses in Scripture: John 3:16. Then we'll look at some of the layers in Colossians 3:1–4.

THE JESUS CORE:

Where do you see the message of Jesus Christ as Savior in John 3:16?

ANOTHER LAYER:

Where can you look back and see the message of John 3:16 working in your childhood?

ANOTHER LAYER:

Where can you see the message of John 3:16 working today in someone else's life?

ANOTHER LAYER:

Where can you see the message of John 3:16 working in your own life today, in this moment?

Layers: it's not just for baklava anymore.

Yesterday we saw the Jesus Core of Colossians 3:1–4: our lives hidden and truly found in Christ.

Today let's peel the onion and notice a couple of the layers of Colossians 3:1–4. We'll look at the layers—that is, the applications to our lives—of seeking and setting.

What are we supposed to seek, according to Colossians 3:1?

What are we supposed to set, according to Colossians 3:2?

Paul states that our life being wrapped up with Jesus is a status that won't change. He exhorts the Colossians and us to seek and set because they are processes that continue throughout our lives.

God's Word is His revelation to us. He makes Himself known to us through His Word, and He continues to teach us and guide us through it. Turning to His Word is part of seeking and setting. Let's turn to His Word right now to better understand what it means to seek and set on our Savior.

Look at the following Scripture passages. What insights related to *seeking* do you find in each passage?

Isaiah 55:6–7

Matthew 6:31–34

Acts 17:24–27

Look at the following Scripture passages. What insights related to *setting* do you find in each passage?

Romans 8:3–6

Mark 8:31–35

Psalm 141:8–10

HINT
Psalm 141 may not use the word *set*, but where do you see the concept of setting on the Lord in this passage?

We know that being in Christ means Jesus has already found us. So it seems a little weird that we are supposed to keep seeking. And yet this is part of the mystery of the Christian life.

Sometimes we call this "the now and not yet."

- We're saved, and we're being saved.
- We're in Christ, and we continue to seek Christ.
- The war has been won, but we're in the spiritual warfare cleanup.
- Our life is with Christ, but it is hidden, so our walk with Him for now is mysterious.
- We know we are already complete through Jesus' death and resurrection, and yet we grow each day.

This "now and not yet" is why even Paul, the great missionary, evangelist, and apostle, speaks of continuing to seek the things that are above during his own life.

Read Philippians 3:7–14. In these verses, how does Paul describe what he is seeking? What was he gaining in his daily seeking and setting with Christ?

ζητέω
zēteō: to seek, search for, desire.[25]

Seeking and setting are more about the desire in our heart than about an action of our hands and feet. It might look like taking on something new that we feel God is asking us to do, or it may look like sitting quietly with God's Word and in prayer and letting Jesus tend to us. Seeking and setting are not restricted to intellectual activities. It can include God working in our emotions and our relationships. It can also include what is physical, like eating Christ's body and blood in the Lord's Supper.

Let's brainstorm: What are some of the many ways God invites us to seek Him and set our minds on Him?

Consider some of the things you listed: how are they holistic, perhaps involving us spiritually, physically, intellectually, emotionally, and even relationally?

Can you incorporate into your life any of these ways of seeking and setting your mind on the things above? If so, brainstorm a plan of how you might do so.

We seek and we set our minds always on Him. He is mighty. He is mysterious. He is Jesus, our Messiah.

CONNECTED BY THE WORD

Use the Scripture memory verse for the week and the prayer prompt to bring your confession, thanksgiving, praise, and requests before our mighty and mysterious God.

WEEK 4 MEMORY VERSE

When Christ who is your life appears, then you also will appear with Him in glory. (Colossians 3:4)

PRAYER PROMPT

Holy Spirit, You point us to Jesus every time we read or hear God's Word. Work in my heart, mind, and life to set my mind on and seek Christ today . . .

Day 5

In July 2010, which now seems epically long ago, our family went on vacation to explore Virginia and Washington, DC. It was a very American history vacation. But I mostly remember three things about the trip:

- Getting rained on to the point of being sopping wet . . . Every. Day.

- My oldest daughter gracefully sliding down a quarter-mile-long rocky hillside at Mount Vernon and scraping herself up enough to need a medic, which then led to a free boat ride down the Potomac. (Score!)

- And water bottles.

Not just any water bottles. "Bottles of Wet Kindness," as I like to call them.

Did I mention it was *July*? Oh! I forgot to mention the detail of my extremely pregnant personhood and how for 99 percent of the day when it wasn't deluging, there were 106°F temperatures with 99 percent humidity. America's national capital was so obscenely hot during that particular week, some very thoughtful government official who really should be nominated for the next presidential bid organized a citywide campaign to hand out free water bottles to people walking around the city. I could not step off a curb without a cab driver or police officer pulling up alongside us and asking, "Would you like some water, ma'am?"

I WOULD!

We live in a very individualistic society. Small acts of kindness like giving water bottles on a hot day become big and significant because this kind of reaching into one another's lives is not something we do or see very often.

Receiving water on those hot, steamy days left me thinking about individualism and our need for community. Sometimes we talk about individualism or our lack of community as if it were a modern problem.

Ecclesiastes 1:9–10 suggests differently. What does this passage say about the issues of individualism and the lack of community in our time versus at other times in history?

Societies tend to swing on a pendulum between a strong focus on community and a strong focus on the individual. And yet even when societies have a strong focus on community, people are still self-centered and selfishly motivated. (Something to do with that blasted fall-into-sin thing.) Our instincts are not only self-serving, but we also default to interpreting everything through our own perspective rather than attempting to walk in someone else's shoes (metaphorically speaking).

Can you think of a situation in which people's selfish nature shows itself?

Because of this selfish state we find ourselves in, combined with our current culture's strong trend toward individualism, when we read Colossians 3:5–12 we most likely read it for ourselves. We ask ourselves, "How have *I* participated in these sins? How is Christ clothing *me* with His righteousness and loveliness?" In next week's study, we will look at Colossians 3:5–12 from this vantage point. But today I want to look at Colossians 3:5–12 from a community vantage point. God cares about individuals *and* He cares about the community. Only God gets the balance perfectly right. As His people, we try to reflect God's balanced care for both as well. Since individuality is our default, let's kick against the grain and start with how the words Paul writes in Colossians 3:5–12 about sin and grace impact our life *together*.

CHRIST HAS CALLED US INTO LIFE TOGETHER. THEREFORE, SIN IS SIN TOGETHER, AND GRACE IS GRACE TOGETHER.

You can take the concept of togetherness too far, of course. We are not saved as a group. We are saved as individuals. There are times when we wish we could repent of sin and find salvation in Jesus on someone else's behalf. But we can't. Christ's death is for everyone, but faith in His death and resurrection brings salvation to each of us as individuals. And yet our faith means that we care about others because Jesus has cared for us. Perhaps the clearest reason why community is so important as believers in Jesus is that we are called the Body of Christ. We belong to Him and to one another.

What are the implications of being part of one Body, the Body of Christ, according to 1 Corinthians 12:20, 24–26?

In the Church, Christ has knit us together in such a way that when one falls, when one sins, we all hurt and we all suffer.

Let's walk through Colossians 3:5–12 verse by verse and consider how sin and redemption affect us together in community. As we look at these verses, you can think about your local congregation, or the larger Church on earth.

Put to death therefore what is earthly in you: sexual immorality, impurity, passion, evil desire, and covetousness, which is idolatry. (Colossians 3:5)

What effect do evil desires, impurity, sexual sins, and covetousness have on a community? In what ways do these sins destroy community?

When these sins rear their ugly heads, what are some ways that healing can come to the Body of believers together?

On account of these the wrath of God is coming. (Colossians 3:6)

Paul's statement might feel harsh to us. But he says it because he wants the Colossians to avoid taking these sins lightly. In the Colossians' culture and in our culture, the trend was and is to take these sins lightly. But God doesn't take them lightly.

How does Revelation 20:11–15 help us understand that God doesn't take sin lightly?

In these you too once walked, when you were living in them. But now you must put them all away: (Colossians 3:7–8a)

The ways of thinking, acting, and treating others that Paul talks about in this section of Colossians are other examples of the thousands of things we die to when we die with Christ. We once were living to these things. But since we have died with Christ, we have died to these things. And we continue to die to them.

What are the consequences in the Church of forgetting that we are all the same: we all once walked in sin, but we all have been saved by Jesus' grace?

anger, wrath, malice, slander, and obscene talk from your mouth. (Colossians 3:8b)

What effect can these sins have on a community?

How does our language and way of communicating in the Body of Christ affect our relationships? How does it create and shape the environment in our community?

Do not lie to one another, seeing that you have put off the old self with its practices (Colossians 3:9)

How do lies and falsehood impact the community of believers?

From what you know from history class or Bible study, how has the Church spoken falsehood at different times in history? What effects have these examples of the Church speaking falsehood had on the world or society outside of the Church?

and have put on the new self, which is being renewed in knowledge after the image of its creator. (Colossians 3:10)

How is being renewed in knowledge the opposite of falsehood and telling lies?

In what way is it true that believers reflect the image of God primarily together, as a community, not primarily as individual believers?

Here there is not Greek and Jew, circumcised and uncircumcised, barbarian, Scythian, slave, free; but Christ is all, and in all. (Colossians 3:11)

What does this mean concerning the prejudices we have against one another in the Church? What kind of prejudices do you see in the Body of Christ today?

Put on then, as God's chosen ones, holy and beloved, compassionate hearts, kindness, humility, meekness, and patience. (Colossians 3:12)

We've talked a lot about how sin affects the community of believers. How do the gifts from the Holy Spirit mentioned here have an effect on the community?

Relationships often seem like more effort than they are worth. It's hard to see how messy we are as the people of God in the Church, in addition to seeing how messy we are as individuals. It can be disconcerting to see how our messiness smears onto one another. The encouragement, though, in our life together is tucked in at the end of our section of verses for today:

Put on then, as God's chosen ones . . .

(Colossians 3:12)

God chose us, even though He knows how messed up we are, and He calls us holy and beloved. Me just as much as you. You just as much as me. The Book of Colossians reminds us we aren't bound together by our good actions, our good communication, and our zeal to care for one another. If we were, our community would fall apart in an instant. But instead we are bound together by Christ and His love. And that makes all the difference.

CHRIST HAS CALLED US INTO LIFE TOGETHER. THEREFORE, SIN IS SIN TOGETHER, AND GRACE IS GRACE TOGETHER.

This is our mighty and mysterious life together.

CONNECTED BY THE WORD

Use the Scripture memory verse for the week and the prayer prompt to bring your confession, thanksgiving, praise, and requests before our mighty and mysterious God.

WEEK 4 MEMORY VERSE

When Christ who is your life appears, then you also will appear with Him in glory. (Colossians 3:4)

PRAYER PROMPT

Lord, You have made us one Body as Your Church. Help us remember that both our sins and the grace You give us affect one another . . .

A Poem

While I was deep in the heart of studying Colossians, our local library held a writing workshop. The purpose of the workshop was only to inspire creativity and get our brain juices flowing. I needed a night out, so I roped my fifteen-year-old and her friend into going with me just for the fun of it. In one of the last projects of the evening, we were challenged to write a poem about a random item we drew from a large picnic basket. I reached into my basket and drew out a shiny gold candleholder. It was a weighty piece and the heaviness felt good in my hands. It seemed to be made with care, rather than being the mass creation of a factory churning out decor every day. The holder was made of three elephant bodies in one congruent circle. I could easily imagine the elephants marching around and around, never letting one member of the circle fall out into the unknown and unsafe, but taking whatever comes into their midst together.

Perhaps this is too deep a reflection for a gold-plated pillar candleholder, intended for an end table in someone's living room. But at the time, when I held that circle of elephants, with the Colossians in the forefront of my mind, I wanted the world to know God designs the best for us. God designs us in community.

COMMUNITY

Candlestick elephants, gold
Marred with time
Marching in community
Telling their story
Trumpets held high

We mark this place with
The rhythm of larger-than-life drumbeats
Reminding the grass, the sky, reminding this place
Power, grace, and tenderness coexist
When we allow them to breathe

Our circle gives space to the afternoon's possibility
Our circle challenges the wild heart to freedom
Our circle invites space to expand and contract
Expand and contract
Into where one is needed and another rests

Gathering hot, stomping dust, flies
Every number matters, every grey fold of leather
Counted
Valued
We breathe in, discovering the flavor of untethered mouths,
wide to the possibility Heaven brings
Together in this circle marred by time, marching in community

Week 5

ALL THAT IS MASTERED

Viewer Guide

VIDEO 5: THE MASTER OF OUR DAYS
COLOSSIANS 3:5–12

VERSES TO BOOKMARK
Colossians 3:5–12

PREEMINENCE
That which is supreme, having inarguable leadership, authority, and superiority; that which completely surpasses all other things. Jesus' preeminence means that He is Lord and Master of the universe and of our hearts and lives.

COLOSSIANS 1:18
"And He is the head of the body, the church. He is the beginning, the firstborn from the dead, that in everything He might be preeminent."

COLOSSIANS 1:17
"And He is before all things, and in Him all things hold together."

AUTHOR'S NOTE
There is a difference between lamenting to God and asking for His judgment on others, and plotting to exact our own judgment in someone's life.

Things like redemption and salvation were _____ _____.

They are _____ ideas.

CONVERSION OF . . . [*]

   our head:

   our heart:

   our purse:

SEE COLOSSIANS 3:5–12.

PUTTING OFF . . .

[*] Luther's description of how God converts our head, our heart, and our purse can be found in R. Scott Rodin, *The Third Conversion* (Colbert, WA: Kingdom Life, 2011).

2 Corinthians 1:3–5
"Blessed be the God and Father of our Lord Jesus Christ, the Father of mercies and God of all comfort, who comforts us in all our affliction, so that we may be able to comfort those who are in any affliction, with the comfort with which we ourselves are comforted by God. For as we share abundantly in Christ's sufferings, so through Christ we share abundantly in comfort too."

FIRST TABLE

First Commandment

Second Commandment

Third Commandment

SECOND TABLE

Fourth Commandment

Fifth Commandment

Sixth Commandment

Seventh Commandment

Eighth Commandment

Ninth Commandment

Tenth Commandment

FIRST-TABLE COMMANDMENTS
Commandments one through three are considered first-table commandments because they describe what should and should not happen in our relationship with God.

SECOND-TABLE COMMANDMENTS
Commandments four through ten are considered second-table commandments because they describe what should and should not happen in our relationships with other human beings. However, all of God's commandments are about honoring Him, because they convey what He, our Creator, says is best.

Discussion Questions

1. What big words or abstract ideas in the Christian faith are hard for you to wrap your mind around?

2. Read Mark 12:28–34. How is "The Lord our God, the Lord is one" the greatest commandment? How does this commandment connect to loving our neighbor?

3. In Colossians 3:5–12, which concrete examples of what it means for Jesus to be the Master caught your attention today? Ask God to transform one area of your life where Jesus as Master can be reflected more fully.

Day 1

THE BEST BATH YOU'VE EVER HAD
COLOSSIANS 3:5–12

Bible study can all at once be exhilarating and exhausting. Slowly walking through a book in Scripture, like we are doing with Colossians, can feel tedious sometimes. But I think there is a lot of payoff, if we're willing to wait to see it. We can discover reflections of God's grace that we haven't ever seen before by taking time to digest small sections of verses and think about how they connect to the rest of that one book, as well as to the rest of the Bible.

I hope you're coming to love Colossians and its intricacies as much as I do. I hope when you have worshiped over the last few weeks, the Colossian Church came to mind. I hope you feel like you know Paul and Timothy a little better than you did before this study. I hope the Early Christian Church feels more like they are part of the Body of Christ with you, rather than a distant group from thousands of years ago. All who are in Christ are the same: saved by grace and each washed by Him.

Today we are looking at Colossians 3:5–12 once more. This passage can speak to each of us differently, depending on the sins we are currently wrestling with, the sins that haunt us from our past, and how the Holy Spirit is working in us today.

Read Colossians 3:5–12. Consider how it speaks to your individual life. Consider what Paul says in light of the fact that Jesus is Lord over our lives and Lord over all. Contemplate how Jesus is working transformation in your life in the following three realms:

Your mind—how is Jesus shaping your mind and fixing it on Him, in light of Colossians 3:5–12?

Your heart—what is God molding and softening in your heart through this passage?

Your actions—how is Jesus showing you that He is Lord of all you do and own according to Colossians 3:5–12? How is He transforming your view of your pocketbook, your home, and your vocations?

This passage makes us think about change.

Colossians 3:8 uses the phrase

"But now . . ."

Those two words signify that something is different between belief and unbelief.

Sometimes, though, we struggle to see any difference. We expect our lives to change drastically after we become Christians. Yet evil things still happen to us when we are Christians. Our neighbors are still rude to us. People still get on our nerves. Our lives are still filled with pain and disappointment. So we're discouraged. Shouldn't being a Christian make my life easier?

GOD DIDN'T PROMISE TO CHANGE OUR CIRCUMSTANCES. HE PROMISED TO CHANGE US.

Sometimes it can seem like a pipe dream—change in the people around us and change in ourselves. We look at our spouse, our family, our boss, and we wonder why in the world they can't be gentler, sprinkle more kindness, not lash out at us. We read in God's Word about nice ideas like holiness and righteousness; but they seem so far out of our reach as we sit in a world broken by sin. We want our neighbor to live more in light of Colossians 3:5–12. And yet simultaneously we see how we ourselves stumble in living out Colossians 3:5–12. We think,

"I wish I could be gentle."

"I wish I was pure."

"I wish I could get my mouth to behave itself."

We—all of us—are a mess. And by "we," I mean humanity—the Colossians, Paul and Timothy, Luther and Melanchthon, Calvin (and Hobbes too), pastors, parents, you, and me. We are a mess.

But what ultimately makes the difference in the end is not who we are, not who our neighbors are, but rather who Christ is.

> **VOCATION**
> A calling, professionally, personally, or in family life. People have many vocations: daughter, brother, husband, mother, teacher, neighbor, friend, business manager, barista, and so forth. These vocations are not our identity but rather areas of life in which we serve and are able to give glory to God. Vocations can change with seasons of life. Our identity never changes: we are children of God, redeemed by Christ Jesus.

When I was in graduate school, I regularly worked with survivors of rape and incest. This is a terribly hard topic for many of us. Survivors who shared their stories with me often mentioned that they would stand in a shower and try to scrub away the stains of iniquity and shame they felt were physically on them from someone else's sexual sin. The presence of sin and evil in the world takes an enormous toll. Jesus Christ sees our struggles and is not deaf to our cries.

We can know clearly and confidently that God has cleansed us once and for all by baptizing us into Jesus' death on the cross. And yet we still need to know that He cleans us every day. Sometimes we are desperate to be cleansed by God each day because we have been the victim of something very dark, such as rape or abuse. Sometimes it is because the grime of sin in our lives or in the world around us makes us feel like this messy broken world, rather than Christ's transforming work, is winning.

Satan's plan is to pillage our lives so that Christ can have no place. Satan weasels his way into our homes and our families in order to destroy. It is right to be angry about this. Satan and his destruction should make us angry. It makes God angry. As Paul says in Colossians 3:6, "On account of these the wrath of God is coming." God holds that anger close, measured, waiting to pour His wrath out at the right time. That means God will do what needs to be done. Ultimately, we can leave it to God to be sufficiently angry about Satan's destruction and the brokenness of the world. We don't need to hang onto our frustration and anger. Instead, we can turn it over to Him in prayer.

CHRIST'S POWER IS STRONGER THAN SATAN'S—EVERY TIME.

In our Baptism, God put to death what is earthly in us (Colossians 3:5) and washed us completely clean. He took all the junk of sin that we have done and that has been done to us, and He washed it and washed it and washed it away through His forgiveness.

The Holy Spirit came into our lives, and He changed us with Jesus' love.

God still cleanses us every day, and as Colossians 3:12 says, the Holy Spirit continues to change us with Jesus' love.

Taking off sin and putting on compassion, kindness, forgiveness, and gentleness is a huge change from who we were before we died with Christ. True, we don't always see the change, but we trust that His washing lasts until eternity. It's the best bath we've ever had and ever will have. And one day He will bring that washing to completion when Jesus returns.

He is Master of our faith and the Master of our days, from day one until eternity. We are not our own master. And our Master is mighty and mysterious and good.

Connected by the Word

Use the Scripture memory verse for the week and the prayer prompt to bring your confession, thanksgiving, praise, and requests before our mighty and mysterious God.

Week 5 Memory Verse

And above all these put on love, which binds everything together in perfect harmony. (Colossians 3:14)

Prayer Prompt

Lord, You are our loving Master. Touch my life with Your grace that I might see how You have washed away my sins . . .

Day 2

DROWNING ALL THE -ISMS
COLOSSIANS 3:8–11

I want the world to be a better place. I'm a social worker. It's part of my psyche to want more and better in this world, to work alongside people toward that goal, and to believe change *can* happen for the better. I want us to get along better together in this world.

I also want my own kids to get along better. But just like change in the world, I'm not fooling myself that it's going to happen overnight. Getting along is hard.

What kinds of things do children argue over?

What kinds of things do adults argue over?

We adults are not all that different from children in the way we treat one another, are we? In Colossians 3, Paul describes what maturity in living out our Christian faith looks like. He exhorts the Colossians to that maturity. This maturity is growth and change that takes a lifetime. Maturity doesn't just show up on our doorstep. If it did, all moms of teenagers everywhere would perpetually be doing a happy dance. Instead, maturity is a work of God in us. The good news is that our salvation doesn't depend on our maturity. It depends on Jesus and only Jesus. But maturing in faith helps us reflect Jesus to the world more clearly, and it better brings love to our neighbor in this troubled world.

Which ways of acting and thinking *go away* as God works maturity in us, according to Colossians 3:8–11?

Which ways of acting and thinking *become part of us* as God works maturity in us, according to Colossians 3:8–11?

Did you notice how the first half of 3:8–11 addresses our tendency to use our words to hurt others? And wow, we can be ever so hurtful to one another with our words. Sticks and stones may break our bones, but words break our hearts and our spirits. These wounds can be some of the most powerful, and sometimes we carry them around for a lifetime after they happen. Anger spewed out all over someone else, malicious statements spoken to someone's face or behind their back, language that shames others—these are not Christ's work in us. Let's take a moment to reflect a little more deeply on these examples of ways we hurt one another. Using a dictionary, the internet, or another resource you find helpful, write down a definition for each of the following ideas from Colossians 3:8–9, and then consider what other words or actions are often associated with them:

Angry words:

EPHESIANS 4:26
How does this verse help us understand what we should do with our anger?

"Be angry and do not sin; do not let the sun go down on your anger."

Wrath:

Malice:

Slander:

Obscene talk:

Lying:

Where do you see any of these kinds of language or talk around you in the world today?

How about in the Church?

When we are tempted to use words in ways that do not show maturity of faith in Christ, whether in our families, in meetings, on social media, or elsewhere, what are some ways we can change our language instead?

When we see the things Paul lists in Colossians 3:8–9 happening in the Church, what are some ways we can respond that reflect Christ instead?

Paul describes one way that we can respond that reflects maturity in Christ. And actually, it's a response that addresses so many of the sins we struggle with.

Here there is not Greek and Jew, circumcised and uncircumcised, barbarian, Scythian, slave, free; but Christ is all, and in all. (Colossians 3:11)

By saying that Christians needed something other than Christ—special knowledge or special rituals and practices, such as worshiping angels and spirits—the false teachers were creating a special group among the Colossian Christians, a group that said they were the *truly* faithful ones. They were dividing the Colossian Christians, labeling people, and making sure that everyone knew some people were better than others.

This is no small problem in our world today as well.

Prejudice is prevalent in our communities, both inside and outside the Church.

Which prejudices can you see in our world today?

As you look at Colossians 3:11 again, are there examples in our world of the prejudices that the Colossian Christians seemed to have been struggling with?

Paul's response to the prejudice dividing the Colossians is brief. But it completely negates any of our reasons for having division among those who trust in Jesus.

What wisdom does Paul give in Colossians 3:11?

This is very clear. There is no confusion here. Being in Christ means no division, no prejudice, no -isms.

Though we are prone to creating division and hurting one another, Christ drowned our hurtful communication and all of our divisions—our sexism, our racism, our ageism, and every other -ism—in our Baptism. He washed us clean.

As Colossians 3:10 says,

[He gave us a] new self, which is being renewed in knowledge after the image of its creator.

(Colossians 3:10)

Renewal came to us in the washing and drowning with the Word in the waters of Baptism. Our new self continues to be renewed every day. Yesterday we talked about how this one washing lasts through eternity. Because of that one washing, God causes our new self to grow and mature each day.

Baptism and life lived in Jesus Christ declare every day:

"Be gone hate!"

"Be gone pride!"

"Be gone prejudice!"

It's a challenge to live in that, to let the new self we received in Baptism work in our lives by the Spirit. It is the work of having hard conversations about sinful things that are difficult to confront, instead of prohibiting or smothering those conversations. Remember that in the Church, when we confront sin and the darkness, the Holy Spirit is always in the room. He doesn't leave, and He will guide us through the tough conversations.

What are some ways we can begin to stand against the prejudices we struggle with in our families, our communities, and our churches?

1 Thessalonians 5:19–24
How do these verses help encourage us as we think about hard conversations in the Church?

"Do not quench the Spirit. Do not despise prophecies, but test everything; hold fast what is good. Abstain from every form of evil. Now may the God of peace Himself sanctify you completely, and may your whole spirit and soul and body be kept blameless at the coming of our Lord Jesus Christ. He who calls you is faithful; He will surely do it."

Hurtfulness, hate, injustice, and prejudice have no place among us. They have no place in me. They have no place in this life lived together in faith in this magnificent community of the Body of Christ.

Unfortunately, the world won't be fully changed and made perfect until Christ comes back. But Jesus works in this world. He drowns all the gunk of our sinful and hurtful ways of speaking with one another and all of our prejudice in His Body. He drowns them mightily and mysteriously through His Spirit. He who promised is faithful. He drowns and drowns and drowns some more.

And in the new self that He raises to life after the drowning, we follow where He leads, reflecting His love to the world in need of true hope, love, and life together.

Connected by the Word

Use the Scripture memory verse for the week and the prayer prompt to bring your confession, thanksgiving, praise, and requests before our mighty and mysterious God.

Week 5 Memory Verse

And above all these put on love, which binds everything together in perfect harmony. (Colossians 3:14)

Prayer Prompt

Lord, drown our prejudice and our hurtfulness today. Especially help me with . . .

Day 3

THE ART OF GETTING DRESSED
COLOSSIANS 3:12–14

The world can be a difficult and divisive place to live. It can also be an exceptionally beautiful place to live. Hearing Paul talk about prejudice and words ill-used in Colossians 3:5–11 might make us want to cringe and likely made the Colossians cringe. We know how often we are guilty of putting on the ugly, divisive things that Paul and the Holy Spirit call us to put off. But in today's reading, Paul shows us the antidote: the beautiful things Christ brings into our lives through His love and forgiveness.

In the space below, note all the things described in Colossians 3:12–14 that Christ offers us:

Colossians 3:12–14 is a reminder that God loves what is hard to love. That is what is so crazy about God's love. He knows that we are all what Paul is talking about in Colossians 3:5–9. And yet He loves us even still. He loves us enough to remove the ugly, filthy, black rags of sin that are our clothes on our own. He removes them with His touch of forgiveness and salvation. And then He helps us get dressed in what is beautiful. As Paul writes in Colossians 3:12, God shows us what to "put on."

When I was in my gap summer between high school and college, I found myself exploring Rome with my mom. Two more determined women have never been found. It was June, hot enough for steam to rise from the pavement, and we only had two days in the city. But nothing was going to stop us from seeing everything. At one point, we took a break from touristing in order to eat giant hunks of crusty bread with peanut butter slathered on them and drink white wine from plastic cups while sitting on the curb of a sidewalk near the Trevi Fountain. While we were eating, a local told us there was a segment of ruins specifically related to the Early Church just a few blocks away, "right at the edge of town." My mom and I only needed to glance at each other to know this *was* going to happen.

Two and a half hours later, dragging empty water bottles and feet sore enough to make actual tears run down our faces, we arrived at the ruins. They were just unspectacular enough that I can't remember where they were, what connection they had to the first three centuries, or what we did when we got there. What I do remember was my poor choice of footwear. I was wearing classic strappy tan leather sandals, fashionable enough for a Roman summer holiday, but not for miles of walking. They were a fine choice for sitting by the Trevi Fountain eating baked goods and drinking wine, or even exploring art museums and cathedrals. But trying to hike across a massive city in them became a cross between *What Not to Wear* and the aftermath of *Jaws*. It was difficult to distinguish between the blisters on my feet and the blood.

As Paul says in Colossians 3:12, God *does* show us how to get dressed. My story about my sandals in Rome is not unlike how we often *try* to get dressed for our Christian walk. We sit by a fountain, just meandering through life, until we hear the Holy Spirit whisper something cool and Jesus-y, and we jump up and plunge in. We end up battered and worn, lamenting our poor decisions and the casualties of bloodied feet and bloodied relationships.

How about you? When have you found yourself with poor "apparel" in a relationship or in a particular conversation?

We forget that God knows what we need for this journey. We forget to ask Him to help us put on what He knows is best for this challenging, tricky, lifelong pilgrimage in Christ. We cannot begin to know what we need in the way that God knows what we need. He proves Himself over and over again to be a good and gracious Father, as well as Lord and Master, by constantly knowing better than us, constantly choosing better for us. Through His Spirit, He layers our relationships with compassion, kindness, and reconciliation when we would accidentally (or even intentionally) walk into anger, malice, and coveting.

But we misunderstand Colossians 3:12–14 if we think God clothes us only with virtues. God's central clothing line is not virtues only. Virtues are good, but they aren't God Himself. Instead of just virtues, God wants us to reflect His very self by reflecting the way He has chosen to make a relationship with Him possible again: through forgiveness.

His forgiveness is the only reason we can have a relationship with Him. It is the only reason we are transformed from what Colossians 3:5–9 describes. And His forgiveness is so powerful that it does in fact change everything. Not only does He show us His forgiveness toward us, but He also shows us that this forgiveness is the only stable foundation for all other relationships.

Fill in the missing pieces of Colossians 3:13 below:

. . . bearing with one another and, if one has a complaint against another, _____ each other; as the Lord has _____ you, so you also must _____.

Forgiveness is the only true apparel that allows us to walk the long journey of this lifetime. And forgiveness is also the foot bath, antibiotic ointment, and foot massage when we choose the wrong apparel. The old man in us wants to wear his own brand of moldy, grimy rags—contempt, disdain, envy, and a tongue that tears others down in order to make ourselves look better. Instead, Jesus dresses us in the beautiful, radiant garment of His forgiveness, adorned with the additional gifts of compassion, kindness, humility, meekness, patience, and love.

Colossians 3:12 says to us:

WE HAVE BEEN LOVED.

WE HAVE BEEN INVITED.

One of my favorite images of how God shows us mercy and kindness and how He dresses us to be in His presence in an ongoing, abiding relationship with Him is from 2 Samuel 9.

Read 2 Samuel 9:1–13. What actions in this story were acts of mercy and grace, forgiveness and compassion?

Picture yourself being like Mephibosheth, but before God instead of David. God invites us not only into His presence, not only to bow down at His feet in order to be near Him; He also invites our crippled selves to come up to His throne and eat at His table for the remainder of our days.

Surely Mephibosheth, crippled in both his feet, was not dressed in garments fit for coming before the king. But David made him fit to appear in the king's presence and made him a guest at the king's table—for the rest of his life. And so God does with us.

God's tender act of dressing us in His forgiveness over and over again is intimate in ways our brains cannot fathom. It goes further than putting a robe on us to distinguish us as family members of the King. It is a daily wrapping us up in His love so that His forgiveness overcomes even the most grotesque parts of who we are and how we act.

What pictures come to mind for you when you think of this imagery for how Jesus bestows His forgiveness and tenderness on you daily?

The wonderful garments Jesus gives us make it possible for us to have the relationship with God that He has wanted ever since Adam and Eve realized they were naked in the Garden of Eden. And He invites us to live in the adventure of that relationship with Him always. The clothing He provides wraps around each of us and also around and between all of our relationships in His Church. Truly, we are His holy and beloved ones—together.

CONNECTED BY THE WORD

Use the Scripture memory verse for the week and the prayer prompt to bring your confession, thanksgiving, praise, and requests before our mighty and mysterious God.

WEEK 5 MEMORY VERSE

And above all these put on love, which binds everything together in perfect harmony. (Colossians 3:14)

PRAYER PROMPT

Lord, dress me in love, dress me in kindness, dress me in Your mercy . . .

Day 4

RULING, DWELLING, AND DOING
COLOSSIANS 3:15–17

In the spring of 2018, our nine-year-old daughter, Jyeva, broke her elbow. Jyeva loves skateboards, her Fender guitar, and anything that remotely sounds challenging. That spring, she "tripped" climbing down the back patio steps. Her climbing method involved hanging like Spider-Man upside down, moving from spindle to spindle. Who would have guessed that was going to go poorly? She found herself in a sling for four weeks with a condylar fracture of the humerus. The next day, I found her skateboarding off the front stoop in her sling and spiky bike helmet, which she told me kept her safe.

An unexpected result of her broken elbow was that Jyeva now needed someone's help to get dressed, much like a toddler. She would come downstairs with a shirt in her hand and a wry look on her face every day, asking me to help her carefully slide her shirt over her head and through the single arm which could still hold a shirt sleeve. Occasionally, I would find her in her room desperately trying by herself to remove one shirt and put on another.

Intimacy is built between people when someone needs help. I wouldn't trade those four weeks of helping Jyeva get dressed for all the sweet tea in Alabama. During that time, we discussed all of the inventions we wished we could make for people with disabilities. We also spent time dreaming about the adventures we could have, even with a broken elbow or a broken leg. Sometimes we ended up so invested in our conversations that we forgot what we were doing. Jyeva would wind up tangled so much in her shirt, we couldn't figure out which way was up. We would giggle so hard that eventually one of us would run away, needing to use the bathroom.

There is a similar sense of intimacy in what Paul describes in Colossians 3:15–17. What intimacy do you hear when you read those verses?

We don't often hear the word *rule* as an intimate word. But in Jesus, the King of kings, suddenly the word *rule* can be understood as a word of grace and love. In Jesus, what seems like a contradiction or an oxymoron can exist in harmony.

How do the following Scripture passages describe Christ as King in very different but complementary ways?

Colossians 1:15–19

Philippians 2:5–11

Jesus is the King who is before all things, but He willingly bent down in humility and compassion to die on a cross for us.

Having a toddler in your house teaches you about bending down. If you want to connect with someone under three feet tall, eventually you have to bend down. While we hesitate to bend down, ruing the effort required to do so, the relationship built with a toddler through bending down is well worth it. The same is true of what Christ accomplished by bending down to us—except that He never hesitated. Ever. He didn't hesitate to bend down to us when He came among us as a helpless infant, and He doesn't hesitate to continue to bend down to us as He is part of our daily lives. Christ's kingship teaches us that ruling is about serving and reaching out, not grabbing power; bending down, not lording over; connecting, rather than remaining far away. Christ's kingship that is both all-powerful and covered in humility is the background for what Paul says about our daily lives in Christ in Colossians 3:15–17.

According to Colossians 3:15, what rules in our hearts because Christ rules the world?

That peace is a gift that is bestowed on us. But sometimes we store it on a shelf in the guest bedroom, as if it were simply a decoration to be brought out for Easter, instead of letting it be part of our daily lives. When that happens, the peace of Christ isn't really ruling.

Look at the other actions Paul mentions in Colossians 3:16–17. How do those actions relate to the peace of God?

Another great word that Paul uses in these verses is *dwell*. Dwelling is when something stays. When we dwell, we are in a particular space for a significant amount of time. We live in that space. It's our address.

Paul urges us to let the word of Christ *dwell* in us.

Who knew? The Bible is for dwelling, not just for reading.

What is the difference between reading the Word and dwelling in the Word?

Many times when we say that we "read the Bible," we don't mean we are only decoding words on a page. So it's not that using the word *reading* is wrong. But the word *dwelling* does give us a fuller description. It's a relational word, a connecting word. It reminds us that Jesus doesn't only give us God's Word. He is God's Word.

DWELLING IN GOD'S WORD IS STAYING PUT IN JESUS.

EVERY TIME WE PICK UP OUR BIBLE, WE PICK UP HIS HAND.

When we pick up our Bible, we sit with Jesus to learn, to grow, to have a conversation with Him, to be listened to, and to listen.

Paul and Timothy tell the Colossians that the Word dwells *richly*. Clearly the Colossians had a desire for richness and abundance in their relationship with God. That's why the false teachers were able to woo the Colossians—the idea of having deeper, stronger, more special knowledge or experiences with God was appealing to them because they were seeking a rich relationship with God.

I can relate to that. I want richness during my short life on this earth too. Most of us would much rather have a feast of diverse and perfectly paired flavors than stale bread and tasteless broth. The Holy Spirit in Colossians 3:16 promises us that the richness or depth we seek in life is found in being in relationship with God through His Word.

Notice, though, in this passage that dwelling in God's Word is not something we do alone:

Let the word of Christ dwell in you richly, _____ and _____ _____ _____ in all wisdom.

So, let's amend our prior statement: The Holy Spirit in Colossians 3:16 promises us that the richness and depth we seek in life and faith is found in being in relationship to God *and one another* through God's Word.

The next statement in Colossians 3:16 takes a turn we might not expect. Fill in the missing words from Colossians 3:16 below to bring out this detail in the passage:

Let the word of Christ dwell in you richly, teaching and admonishing one another in all wisdom, _____ _____ and _____ and _____ _____, with _____ in your hearts to God.

Music is a powerful thing, a unique gift from God. In particular, music can span cultural distinctions, language barriers, and differences in life experience to connect people.

What is your relationship with music? Has music ever helped you connect with another person?

Why do you think Paul gives music such a high place in our life together in Christ in Colossians 3:16?

How are psalms, hymns, and spiritual songs connected to the Word of Christ dwelling in us richly?

Can you think of a time when psalms, hymns, and/or spiritual songs helped you express gratitude to God?

Ruling and dwelling lead to our final word for today, something really awesome: *doing*. After verse 17, the rest of Colossians 3 addresses doings of many different kinds: in our homes, with our neighbors, and in our communities. What is true in all of those examples, though, is that our doing is before God—and in the name of our Lord Jesus.

Sometimes we prematurely jump to descriptions of doing because those are concrete, and we like clear, concrete instructions. Doing is good. But Colossians 3:15–17 says the doing comes out of Christ's ruling and our dwelling in Him. We can't have the doing without the ruling and the dwelling. Without the ruling and the dwelling, doing is just a bunch of checkmarks on our to-do list. God cares about our souls more than our to-do lists. Because He is the King and He is our Master, His peace rules in our hearts. He gives us the gift of dwelling together in His Word. Our doing yesterday, today, tomorrow, and forever finds meaning and completion in Him.

Connected by the Word

Use the Scripture memory verse for the week and the prayer prompt to bring your confession, thanksgiving, praise, and requests before our mighty and mysterious God.

Week 5 Memory Verse

And above all these put on love, which binds everything together in perfect harmony. (Colossians 3:14)

Prayer Prompt

Lord, You have my heart. Rule, dwell, and do in me today . . .

Day 5

MASTER OF OUR HOUSE, KEEPER OF OUR ZOO
COLOSSIANS 3:18–4:1

The entire Letter of Colossians has bordered on excessively abstract until our text for today. We have talked about many mysterious things: false teaching, meta, mind-blowing concepts like preeminence. But today's course in Colossians' mighty and mysterious banquet of ideas is the very practical meat of daily life. Remember Colossians 3:17 from yesterday?

And whatever you do, in word or deed, do everything in the name of the Lord Jesus, giving thanks to God the Father through Him.

(Colossians 3:17)

Colossians 3:18–4:1 describes how "whatever you do" might look in life. This segment identifies some of the major roles and vocations of Paul's hearers in first-century Asia Minor. And yet these core vocations have existed in nearly every society ever, including our own. Today let's work through this list of admonishments (warnings or reproaches) and encouragements to find some straightforward wisdom for our families, our relationships, and our lives.

Read Colossians 3:18–4:1 and list every role and vocation Paul addresses. Also note any modern, alternative expressions of each role or vocation (such as stepmom or boss):

AUTHOR'S NOTE

If one of these roles or vocations is not your role, if several of them are not your role, they still do touch you in some way, because we are all knitted together, pieced together in this Body of Christ. He is the Master of the house, the Keeper of the zoo, and we are all an important part of it, an important part of one another.

When I read this list in Colossians 3:18–4:1, it makes me think of a naval crew, in their pristine white uniforms, all perfectly in a line, waiting for instructions. Nice, neat, and orderly, waiting to be addressed. And they each receive their instructions in turn: "Wives, do this. Husbands, do this. Children, do this. That is your assignment, now move along the line. Next, please." My household, my life, on the other hand feels more like a zoo or a trip to the circus than a nice, neat, tidy, well-ordered phenomenon like what Paul and Timothy describe. Order is good. God is a God of order. But God is also a God of grace. If we were perfect, if the world was perfect, our lives would be perfectly ordered. But we are not and they are not.

Name an example from the last week in which you had structured and ordered plans, but your plans did not pan out.

LIFE WILL BE MESSY UNTIL JESUS COMES BACK.

BUT JESUS PROMISES HE MAKES OUR MESS BEAUTIFUL.

Christ brings order to our chaos. It doesn't mean the chaos and the mess completely go away. But when we are in Christ, He becomes the Master of our house, the Keeper of our zoo. And when He is the Master of the house, the Keeper of the zoo, He gently guides us in what is good, so that even in the mess and chaos, there is joy and life in Him—even on the days when it feels like you're the pooper-scooper at the zoo.

That's the way Paul intends us to hear Colossians 3:18–4:1. Not as marching orders on a tightly run ship, but as thoughtful, caring guidance for life in the zoo. For the rest of today's study, read the verse listed next to each bolded role or vocation. What follows in each case are some of my thoughts. Write down and reflect on your own thoughts as you encounter each verse, or use the questions I offer for further consideration.

WIVES—COLOSSIANS 3:18

Nothing like starting with an awkward example right out of the gate, Paul. These words can be hard to hear sometimes. But as we hear them, it's helpful to remember that in God's economy, there is no inferiority even within the concept of submission. If inferiority is insinuated or overtly expressed when we read or hear about wives submitting to their husbands, that idea

AUTHOR'S NOTE
When I hear the word *submission*, it's unfortunate that domestic violence immediately comes to mind. But it does—and it's important that we are honest about that. Domestic violence happens because we live in a sinful world. If either or both spouses in a marriage bring emotional, verbal, mental, or physical abuse into the environmental landscape of their marriage and family life, it is time to visit a pastor, a licensed counselor, or both. If you or someone you know is in danger, please contact the domestic violence hotline by going to thehotline.org.

has been added by the world to the concept of submission. We know that in God's economy there is no inferiority in submission because Jesus lovingly submitted to His Father's will when He redeemed us. Doing so did not make Jesus inferior to His Father.

Our attempts at creating order ourselves, without Christ, will always still be disorder. When I read this verse, it helps me to remember that Jesus is the Master, first and foremost, over both husband and wife. That is why submission is "fitting in the Lord." Seeing my husband's deep expressions of love for me in our day-to-day life together makes putting my strong opinions aside a little easier when it's necessary for me to do so. When my husband makes decisions that I feel lack Christlike love, leading me and our family imperfectly, Christ still is the Master over each of us, our marriage, our family, and our whole house. And He always rules in perfect love. Because Jesus' rule and love are over both of us, I rest in what Jesus is doing in the middle of our zoo, rather than use the occasional messiness we each bring to our marriage as an excuse for not submitting to my husband.

What do you think? How do you see Jesus Christ working as Master of our homes and lives through the role of wife?

HUSBANDS—COLOSSIANS 3:19

When comparing love and submission in marriage, it has been said that love is hardest. I say baloney. They are both hard. Marriage is hard. What is so encouraging, though, is God's ability to just *know*—to know where we are all at, and to know what will bring us trouble, whether we live in the first century or the twenty-first century. God's direction for husbands is to love, but what God says next to husbands shows how well He knows us as human beings:

And do not be harsh with them. (Colossians 3:19)

Harshness does not speak love. Harshness hurts. And yet harshness can be our default, in our sin.

God is not harsh with us. He gets angry. He demands justice. He even addresses us with sternness in His Word. But harshness is not part of His vocabulary.

However, we have a tendency to be harsh with one another. Harshness can look like strong words, inappropriate jokes, or sarcasm at another's expense, or it can look like the silent treatment, ignoring, zoning out, avoiding, and withholding affection. Recognizing what looks, sounds, and feels harsh in your relationships is important.

When we are harsh in our relationships, it is helpful to read God's Word and notice His words, His tone, His attitude, and His actions toward His people. God is the perfect communicator, and His Spirit helps change us to be more like Him in the way we treat one another. As we read His Word, it works in us to mysteriously transform us and our attitudes in mighty ways. This is especially comforting when we know we sin against others through harshness, but we don't know how to transform ourselves.

What speaks harshness in your marriage or relationships? How do you respond to harshness from others?

CHILDREN—COLOSSIANS 3:20

Raise your hand if you were slightly challenging as a child.

Heidi raises her hand. "Oooo, ooo, me! Me! Me!"

Some of us are more easily moldable than others. James Dobson's *The Strong-Willed Child* was a groundbreaking resource when it came out in 1985. Parents everywhere let out a giant sigh of relief as they came to know that they weren't the only ones. God knew, though. God has always known that parents desire to help their squirrely children. And God has always known that we're all a little squirrely, regardless of whether we are children or adults. Whether we are very moldable as children or more resistant to teaching, we are all sinners. And as a result, learning obedience is a challenge.

What do you think are some of the hardest lessons for children to learn?

How do each of those lessons mirror something adults continue learning in their walk?

Still, God showers us with His mercy and grace in Jesus. Without the forgiveness and mercy of God found in Jesus' cross for each and every one of us, being a child can be especially hard. God is at work in a child's life, just as He is at work in us as adults. Jesus makes a difference in children's daily walk too. With Jesus in their lives, children have a sense of safety. They know they are forgiven, loved, and cared for—even when life is messy—because they have a mighty Savior, Jesus, who is the Master over all things.

FATHERS/PARENTS—COLOSSIANS 3:21

Paul's warning about harshness in marriage is similar to what he says about the responsibility of fathers (and by extension, parents). One of my psychology professors in college used to frequently remind us, "Parents do the best they can with the resources they have available at any given time." This grace-based approach to viewing our family of origin can be difficult, because as adults, we often begin to see how our family of origin has lasting effects on our lives. When harshness reigns in a child's environment, it is likely that the child will become an adult who is similarly harsh, controlling, and reactive. Discouragement has powerful effects on children too. Children who consistently see that they disappoint people or are not given room to grow and ask questions are more likely to distance themselves from meaningful relationships and connections.

How have you experienced discouragement in the family you grew up in, your family of origin, specifically? As you reflect on that, try to keep in mind what my professor said: "Parents do the best they can with the resources they have available at any given time."

What hope does 2 Corinthians 1:3–5 give when we are discouraged?

SLAVES—COLOSSIANS 3:22

Slavery is a hot-button word—and rightfully so. The term *bondservant* in the ESV's translation of Colossians 3:22, instead of *slave*, more accurately represents the social conditions Paul and Timothy were addressing in Colossae. At the time of the New Testament, it was legal for someone to become a slave in order to pay off a debt. However, people also became slaves through the conquest of their homeland or through other less than stellar or downright wrong situations. Some masters cared for their bondservants, holding an employer-employee kind of relationship with them. Other masters were cruel and unjust. Still others were harsh or abusive.

Slavery of any kind is never the ideal. The ideal in life is equality for all people. We are all created in God's image, and He shows no partiality.

When I read Colossians 3:22, the message that comes to mind is that even when the system is unjust, there is a way to reflect Christ, even as we work toward changing the broken system. There's a letter in the New Testament to a man named Philemon that was also written by Paul and was likely delivered around the same time as the Letter to the Colossians was delivered. Paul's Letter to Philemon also addressed a situation involving a master and a slave (Onesimus). We will talk more about that letter and its message during the next week of our study. For now, though, it is helpful to know that Paul's Letter to Philemon gives us an additional glimpse into Paul's approach to slavery in the New Testament. The Letter to Philemon clarifies that Paul's message in Colossians 3 is *not* that slavery is good. Rather, his focus is on how believers are called to act justly, even when others do not. Colossians 3:23–25 follows right on the heels of Paul's statement to bondservants because those verses are encouragement for when injustice is thrown in our faces. This is a prime example of why it is important to read Scripture verses within their context.

How is Colossians 3:23–25 encouraging for those who are experiencing injustice or discouragement, especially in their employment, in their community relationships, or because of unjust laws or circumstances?

MASTERS—COLOSSIANS 4:1

Paul and Timothy are careful to address both parties in the relationships they mention in Colossians 3:18–4:1: wives, but also husbands; children, but also parents; slaves, but also masters. Regardless of our place or vocations, God calls each of us who are in Christ to uphold the Word in the way that is fitting for our vocation, in our specific community and our specific time. This section of verses also shows that we are intended to work together as we strive to live in perfect harmony, bound together by love. We were made for one another. Wives complement husbands and husbands complement wives. Parents complement children and children complement parents. The Word of God also instructs us that some vocations are meant to have more authority in certain situations so that there is good order in society and in our life together within the Church. Here is the important distinction though: some people are masters for a moment, while Jesus is the Master over all of us, always.

What responsibility does Colossians 4:1 bestow on anyone who is in charge of anything?

What are you in charge of, or whom do you have influence over? How does Colossians 4:1 apply to you?

Because we are sinners, we are going to struggle to live in the way Paul describes in Colossians 3:18–4:1. Jesus does live in and through us in our families, at our jobs, with our neighbors, among our church community, and anywhere else we go. But we will still be imperfect until Christ comes back. Colossians 3:18–4:1 is about this imperfectly beautiful life we live together. Notice how the focus of this passage is not our perfection. The focus is Jesus as our loving, kind, and just Master. He is the mighty, mysterious, magnificent, majestic, glorious, gracious, faithful, supreme, merciful Master of our beautifully messy days—today and every day.

CONNECTED BY THE WORD

Use the Scripture memory verse for the week and the prayer prompt to bring your confession, thanksgiving, praise, and requests before our mighty and mysterious God.

WEEK 5 MEMORY VERSE

And above all these put on love, which binds everything together in perfect harmony. (Colossians 3:14)

PRAYER PROMPT

Lord, You are Master of this day and the next and every day that has ever existed. Take all I touch today, every relationship I have, and make it beautiful in Your way . . .

Slavery, the Early Church, and the Roman Empire

Karl E. Baughman, PhD
Assistant Professor of History | Prairie View A&M University | kebaughman@pvamu.edu

It is difficult for many to imagine slavery apart from their own nation's history. The slavery with which most are familiar is associated with the enslavement of Africans during the conquest of the Americas and is invariably tied to race. For most Americans, slavery conjures images of the US Civil War (1861–65) and the subsequent issues of racism and regional politics. With all this baggage, encountering passages within Scripture that deal with slavery can make us uncomfortable, or even worse, lead us to doubt the Bible's relevance and authority. Slavery in the New Testament requires some historical context to better understand how and why early Christians, like Paul, engaged with slavery as they did.

The Greek word used in Colossians 3, δοῦλος (*doulos*), is a rather broad concept and is therefore mostly dependent upon context. The typical translations are "slave," "bondservant," and sometimes just "servant." Within the context of Colossians, the translation is most certainly "slave." In the Roman Empire of the first century AD (the time period in which Paul is living and writing), slavery is a part of society that few people would question. It is likely that slaves accounted for about 10 percent of the entire population of the Roman Empire, and perhaps even as high as 35 percent in Italy. This estimate places the slave population at about six million during the first century AD. Unlike the slavery of the later fifteenth to nineteenth centuries, however, Roman slavery was not confined to a particular ethnicity, race, geographic location, education, or level of wealth. Even the process of enslavement could vary. While many were enslaved because they had been captured in war, still a great number were enslaved by pirates and then resold, enslaved as part of criminal punishment, entered slavery to satisfy a debt, or were simply born into slavery. The lives of slaves varied greatly as well. Slaves in the Roman Empire had a variety of educational backgrounds and performed duties ranging from bookkeepers to teachers to physicians to domestic servants to field hands. Despite their abilities, however, slaves were still property and could be violently disciplined or sexually exploited at the will of the master.

Understanding the pervasiveness of slavery in society and the potential for masters to be overly harsh or abusive, Paul included exhortations in his letters for masters to be kind to their slaves (see Ephesians 6:9; Colossians 4:1). These passages are just a few of the numerous references to slavery within the New Testament. Just like the rest of Roman society, slavery permeated early Christian communities as well. Many important early Christians were slaveholders or slaves themselves, many of whom we meet in Acts (chapters 10; 12; 16). It is also reasonable to assume that any Christian wealthy enough to own a large home for early Christian gatherings would also have likely owned slaves. Admonitions to slaves to be obedient and submissive to their masters (Ephesians 6:5; Colossians 3:22; 1 Timothy 6:1; 1 Peter 2:18; Titus 2:9–10) are sprinkled alongside those encouraging masters to be humane to their slaves throughout the letters of Paul and Peter. In the Book of Philemon, Paul encourages Philemon to take back his slave Onesimus, and to "welcome him as [he] would welcome [Paul]" (Philemon 17 [NIV]). In none of these passages do the authors tell masters to free their slaves, nor do they tell slaves to demand their freedom. Instead, each person is encouraged to remain "in whatever condition each was called" (1 Corinthians 7:20–24), though Paul does say to slaves, "If you can gain your freedom, avail yourself of the opportunity" (1 Corinthians 7:21).

This can be disconcerting to today's reader, but as modern Christians, we should remember that the purpose of many of these letters is not to urge the Christian community to any particular action regarding slavery, but rather to remind them that before God, all people—whether slave or free—stood equally sinful and equally redeemed (1 Corinthians 12:13; Galatians 3:28). This is not to say that God does not desire Christians to pursue issues of social justice (cf. Psalm 82:3; Proverbs 31:8–9; Isaiah 1:17; Micah 6:8; Zechariah 7:9–10; Luke 10:30–37; Romans 12:15–18; James 1:27; 1 John 3:17–18). In the context of the first-century Roman Empire however, slavery was a component of stratified society that was devoid of the racial aspects of the later slavery of the Americas. The New Testament writers, while cognizant of the un-Christian facets of slavery, were more focused on emphasizing the revolutionary nature of God's grace that could break down the human divisions in His presence (Galatians 3:28), rather than in advocating any revolutionary political action.

See these resources for more on slavery in the Roman Empire and Early Christianity:

Bradley, Keith. *Slavery and Society at Rome*. Cambridge: Cambridge University Press, 1994.

Glancy, Jennifer. "Slavery and the Rise of Christianity." In *The Ancient Mediterranean World*, edited by Keith Bradley and Paul Cartledge, 456–81. Vol. 1 of The Cambridge World History of Slavery. Cambridge: Cambridge University Press, 2011.

Joshel, Sandra R., and Lauren Hackworth Petersen. *The Material Life of Roman Slaves*. Cambridge: Cambridge University Press, 2014.

Morley, Neville. "Slavery under the Principate." In *The Ancient Mediterranean World*, edited by Keith Bradley and Paul Cartledge, 265–86. Vol. 1 of The Cambridge World History of Slavery. Cambridge: Cambridge University Press, 2011.

Scheidel, Walter. "The Roman Slave Supply." In *The Ancient Mediterranean World*, edited by Keith Bradley and Paul Cartledge, 287–310. Vol. 1 of The Cambridge World History of Slavery. Cambridge: Cambridge University Press, 2011.

Week 6

ALL THAT IS MEANINGFUL

Viewer Guide

VIDEO 6: THE CARE AND FEEDING OF THE CHURCH
COLOSSIANS 4:2–18

PHILIPPIANS 3:8, 10
"Indeed, I count everything as loss because of the surpassing worth of knowing Christ Jesus my Lord . . . that I may know Him and the power of His resurrection."

JOHN 17:3
"And this is eternal life, that they know You, the only true God, and Jesus Christ whom You have sent."

This mighty and mysterious God is a God of _____.

The Church is a community of _____ _____ in life together.

Relationships need to be _____, and genuine community needs to be _____ _____.

NOURISHMENT OF THE CHURCH

- The Word of God, which we also call Scripture or the Bible
- Baptism, the Lord's Supper, and the forgiveness of sins
- Life together with other Christians—including speaking God's Word to one another, knowing one another, and coming together in prayer

SEE COLOSSIANS 4:2–18.

MARKS OF THE CHURCH
If you are curious as to why the Word, the Sacraments, and life together with other Christians are the specific gifts God uses to nourish the Church, see the footnote below.*

TRADEMARKS OF KNOWING

1. _____

IDEAS

- Saying hello to someone new
- Starting conversations and asking questions that aim to get to know a person—what really makes him or her tick
- Hearing one another's stories
- Reaching out and asking without judgment when someone seems to be struggling
- Offering tangible help that takes time, energy, and resources

---

* See the Book of Concord, Smalcald Articles, Part III, Article IV.

-
-
-
-

2. _____

Isolation affects everything: our mental, physical, emotional, and relational health.[**]

Therefore, God gives us the incredible gift in the Church of _____ together—carrying one another's load and sharing the burden.

3. _____

This is the _____ of Christ at work: sharing encouragement back and forth, and then going out into the world by the strength of our relationships with one another and with Jesus.

COLOSSIANS 1:24
"Now I rejoice in my sufferings for your sake."

1 CORINTHIANS 12:12, 24–26
"For just as the body is one and has many members, and all the members of the body, though many, are one body, so it is with Christ. . . . But God has so composed the body, giving greater honor to the part that lacked it, that there may be no division in the body, but that the members may have the same care for one another. If one member suffers, all suffer together; if one member is honored, all rejoice together."

DISCUSSION QUESTIONS

1. What would the Church look like if noticing, suffering, or encouraging—the trademarks of life together that we talked about from Colossians 4—were missing?

2. What are some church memories you treasure?

3. What might you add to the list of trademarks of our life together as the Body of Christ besides noticing, suffering, and encouraging? How is Christ our leader as we do these things?

[**]   Lena Aburdene Derhally, "The Growing Problem of Social Isolation and What to Do about It," updated May 6, 2017, https://www.huffingtonpost.com/lena-aburdene-derhally/the-growing-problem-of-so_b_9847990.html.

Day 1

PRAY IT UP
COLOSSIANS 4:2–4

When I was in high school, one of my English teachers used to stand at the door of the classroom to greet us one at a time. He would very formally acknowledge our arrival with a nod of his head and slowly address us by our last names, as if reminding us of the gravity and dignity of the content we were about to encounter in that day's lesson. I can still see him nod and say my name: "Ms. Weirich." Then, as the bell rang, he would methodically slip his foot under the kickstand door stop and bring the door to a close with the neat click of the latch. This motion signified *the beginning*—the beginning of vibrant discussion, deep contemplation, and open conversation exploring the meaning of great literature.

In Mr. McKee's class, the goal was for us to practice and respect the art of interpretation. Therefore, you were allowed to be wrong because the answers weren't always clean-cut. And that goal was something better and longer lasting than simply having the "right" answers. When his door shut, we also knew we were in a place of safety. Mr. McKee would never allow someone to make fun of another person's thoughts. But he also didn't allow outlandish proclamations of truth that could not be supported. When people said something like that, they were kindly asked to reconsider, to find evidence to support their claims, and to wrestle more deeply with their statements. Mr. McKee shared his thoughts and wisdom about the literature and topics being discussed, but his comments always served to foster discussion, not end it. You never felt like you were on the outside of knowledge. Rather, you felt like you were on the inside, part of knowledge developing as we processed together.

Colossians 4:2 through the end of the Letter to the Colossians feels to me very much like when I heard the door click closed in Mr. McKee's classroom. At first glance, this chapter in Scripture may seem like a long list of names we can skim through quickly or simply write off. In actuality, at this point in the letter, Paul is like a Mr. McKee to the Colossians and to us as believers. Here, Paul models for the Colossians a perspective that sees how the mighty and mysterious God is at work in their circumstances. Paul supports and fosters the Colossians to have the same perspective through his modeling and guidance. In particular, Paul wants the Colossians to see God at work in their specific relationships in the local body of believers and in the specific events happening around them. In a similar way, Paul also models and then leads *us* into a safe but open discussion of how our mighty and mysterious God is at work in our place and time, in our local body of believers, and in Christ's Body around the world now.

One of the ways Paul does this is by starting with how the mighty and mysterious God uses prayer. So that is what we'll focus on for today.

Heidi's paraphrase of Paul's exhortations in Colossians 4:2–4 is this:

PRAY IT UP, COLOSSIANS. PRAY IT UP.

Paul mentions prayer near the very beginning and near the very end of his Letter to the Colossians.

Look at the following passages about prayer. What do you think Paul is teaching the Colossians about prayer in each passage?

Colossians 1:3–4

Colossians 1:9

Colossians 4:2–4

Colossians 4:12

Notice that Paul begins Colossians by talking about "we" in prayer. He ends also by talking about "us" in prayer. Community is at the heart of prayer.

We often think of faith and prayer in particular as being very private things. However, Scripture always shows prayer as being communal. Even when a person is completely alone, his prayers connect him to God and to the Body of Christ, his fellow believers.

Perhaps the strongest example of a person alone in prayer, by all appearances, is Jesus' time of prayer in the Garden of Gethsemane before He allowed Himself to be arrested, hung on the cross, and killed. But . . .

Read Matthew 26:36–46. In what ways was Jesus very much alone? In what ways was Jesus still connected to His Father, to His disciples, and to each of us in His prayers?

How can the truth that prayer is always communal be encouraging to Christians who feel very alone at a particular stage or place in their life?

When Paul asks the Colossians to pray in Colossians 4:2–4, his statements are meant for individuals as well as the community, and the individual applications of his words also affect the community. In these verses, Paul and Timothy exhort the Colossians to pray with watchfulness and with thanksgiving. They exhort the Colossians to pray for themselves, for the relationships among them, for Paul and Timothy, and for God to provide opportunities for people to hear the Word. The longer you look at these verses, the more prayer requests you find.

Every single aspect of this life together begins and ends with prayer according to Paul.

Prayer is all at once challenging and simple. Paul instructs the Colossians to "continue steadfastly in prayer" according to the ESV translation of Colossians 4:2. The NIV translation says Paul encourages the Colossians to "devote [themselves] to prayer." We might not notice it at first, but words like *steadfast* and *devotion* reflect how difficult it can be for us to pray. They are words of perseverance.

In Psalm 130:5–8, the term *steadfast* also appears in the context of prayer. As you read the passage, what deep emotion or truth in these verses encourages you to persevere in presenting your needs, requests, confession, and thanksgiving before God?

The wording of Psalm 130 differs slightly between the ESV and the NIV translations. Look at Psalm 130:5 in both translations below, and circle any differences in the wording of the verse.

ESV	NIV
I wait for the LORD, my soul waits,	I wait for the LORD, my whole being waits,
and in His word I hope.	and in His word I put my hope.

Oooooo, those are both good. But we don't need to choose between the two.

In each translation, what is encouraging to you concerning your own time in prayer?

Both Paul and the psalmist connect watchfulness with prayer. How do watchfulness and prayer go hand in hand?

Where and how do you see steadfastness, perseverance, and watchfulness at work in life together in the Body of Christ? Write your answers in the chart below.

STEADFASTNESS, PERSEVERANCE, AND WATCHFULNESS

As an individual:	
With a few others:	
Among the whole Body of believers:	

The perseverance of prayer with watchfulness is like a race. But it's not a handoff relay: I pray, then you pray, then someone else, and then back to me. Prayer in the Body of Christ is like a giant clump of marathon runners, their own breaths rhythmically flowing in and out, their own feet pounding against the pavement. But they are also aware of the people running beside them, in front of them, and behind them. For many runners, this pack of people around them all going the same direction gives them invisible strength.

How have you experienced this invisible strength of the other runners around you going the same direction in this walk of faith?

What does Paul specifically ask the Colossians to pray for in Colossians 4:3–4?

As Paul sits in prison, we can imagine he probably felt pretty alone. But Paul knows the prayers of his fellow believers connect him to them and will encourage him and strengthen him. Therefore, he asks the Colossians to pray for him, for Timothy, and for the others who are with Paul, even as Paul started his letter by telling the Colossian Christians that he prays for them always.

Amazingly, Paul's request is that the Colossians would pray for a repeat of the very events that put him in prison in the first place: that the Gospel would go out, that the mystery of Christ would be declared, and that the mystery would be made clear—not tripped up by either false teachers or Paul's own words.

Paul's request shows what really matters. In this marathon that we are running together, we can pray for food on our tables, for good health, for our families, for words that won't injure, for justice and peace in our world, but what matters most is that the mystery of Jesus as the Savior of the world is proclaimed to every beating heart.

What is our purpose in this world as believers in Jesus, according to Jesus' prayer for the Church in John 17:20–23?

So in a sense, when we pray the same things, we are simply echoing our Savior's prayers. Therefore, Paul's encouragement and invitation to prayer for the Colossians and us in Colossians 4:2–4 are also Jesus' words to us. Talk about a mighty and mysterious connection!

As a reminder that *you* are part of that connection, write your name in the blank below. Then read the statement aloud (to yourself, or to whomever you are studying with) as an encouragement and invitation to run alongside your fellow believers in this one Body of Christ, fed and nourished by His grace and steadfast love.

Pray it up, _____ . Pray it up.

CONNECTED BY THE WORD

Use the Scripture memory verse for the week and the prayer prompt to bring your confession, thanksgiving, praise, and requests before our mighty and mysterious God.

WEEK 6 MEMORY VERSE

Continue steadfastly in prayer, being watchful in it with thanksgiving. (Colossians 4:2)

PRAYER PROMPT

Jesus, Savior, Friend, I come before You in prayer to enjoy Your company, to honor Your name, and to join with the whole Body of Christ. I ask that You strengthen the connections between the members in Your Body. And I ask that You open doors for us to make Your mighty mercy known to the world . . .

Day 2

SALTY TONGUES
COLOSSIANS 4:2–6

I have two main principles for communication in life:

1. Speak truth in wild amounts of love.

2. Do not ask women about pregnancy unless they themselves have told you they are pregnant.

I find that almost all communication snafus fall under one of these two headings.

Example snafus related to principle 1:

🙁 A woman telling me after a keynote address that I could stand to do with a new hairstyle that would make me look more mature.

🙁 A church member stopping me in the narthex after church and asking why in tarnation I couldn't make my nine-year-old sit still during worship.

Believe it or not, these two less-than-helpful interactions could have been prevented and considerable hurt avoided if communication principle 1 had been used.

Principle 1 tries to reflect how God communicates with us. He is the master communicator. Truth is as important as love, for sure. But Scripture shows us that God pours out wild amounts of love as He communicates truth to us. He communicates truth in the context of a loving and secure relationship with us. As a result, He communicates truth in a way that we can hear it.

I also think it reflects the heart of God to not ask a woman about being pregnant if we don't have prior knowledge of the situation.

I jest, but seriously, sometimes we assume it's okay for us to ask about intimate things even though we haven't been invited into a person's life or into a particular aspect of his or her life. Even in our closest relationships, some things are none of our business, unless we are invited into that business. God is *always* invited into our business because He knows us first, fullest, and deepest. But the uniqueness of His relationship with each human being means He teaches us to care for others lovingly by stepping back, respecting their business, and waiting to be invited into it. Yes, we spend time with people to deepen our relationship with them, and we ask questions as we get to know them; but speaking truth in love also means giving people a choice of whether they want to share with us or not.

My two principles for communication don't come only out of experiences when I was the recipient of grievous statements; they're also out of times when I was the source of embarrassingly grievous statements. When we first moved to Nebraska, I tried to make deep and meaningful friendships instantly with everyone in my path. I'll be upfront: moving has always been difficult for me. The worst part of moving for me is leaving my people for a new location where I know no one. So, in this move to Nebraska, I wanted to have people in this new place, and I felt at a loss for how to get them and get them quickly. But newsflash: deep and meaningful friends rarely come "quickly," and when you try too hard, you will end up with your foot so deep in your throat it may set your BFF search back a few months.

At the grocery store I had been frequenting since we moved, I found myself checking out with the same grocery store checker every week. She is patient, kind, and a good conversationalist. Read that last sentence as, "She seemed like prime friend material." We chatted and laughed about what people buy, what's on sale in the store, what we like to eat, and our husband's/fiancé's TV-viewing habits. In an attempt to take our relationship to a deeper level, in a rash and not-well-thought-out moment, I broke Heidi's communication principle 2. I blurted out, "Are you pregnant?!"

She was not.

What was I thinking?!?!?!

Clearly I *wasn't* thinking. Thankfully, she was kind about my lapse of mental prowess. She had grace when I lacked any form of it. I apologized, and it was awkward for a few weeks after that. But eventually my mistake faded. And when she did find herself pregnant, she joyfully shared her news with me in the same checkout line where I had previously eaten my words.

Have you ever had a foot-in-mouth moment? If so, how was it healed?

Read Colossians 4:2–6. Think outside of the box a bit with me today: what might these verses have to do with asking possibly-not-pregnant women whether they are pregnant?

PICTURE THIS
If it helps, you can imagine communication as a cord that runs between and around me, you, Jesus, God the Father, and the people all around us, connecting our lives to one another.

We easily disconnect our communication with others from the prayer life we talked about yesterday in Colossians 4:2–4. We also think of our daily tasks, like buying milk, sending an email, or sitting in traffic, as being disconnected from the work of sharing Jesus. Just as none of us are islands, completely separated from other human beings, neither is our communication compartmentalized. Our communication with God in prayer, our communication with others throughout our day, and the communication of the Gospel connect and are related to one another—sometimes clearly and sometimes more mysteriously.

How does God's communication with us through His Word and our communication with Him in prayer connect and relate to our communication with others and our tasks in our daily lives?

AUTHOR'S NOTE
Let me be clear that nowhere in the Bible do we explicitly read that you shouldn't ask women about pregnancy unless they tell you they're pregnant. I offer my principles as nice suggestions, not biblically mandated truth!

I have my two general communication principles. What do you think Paul would include in a list of general communication principles?

Communication is hard in life. And that doesn't change in the Body of Christ. We really want communication in the church to be easy. After all, the church is a safe community among fellow believers, right?

And yet why is communication in our life together in the very place God intended for us so difficult?

The community of the Body of Christ *is* safe. But being safe means being more authentic than we are when we're outside of this community. And being more authentic means our broken parts are visible too. Ah, it's messy, friends!

What makes the Body of Christ different from any other community where we might look for relationships is that, here, Christ Himself wraps His love around us and delivers truth to us. He wildly embraces us, His Church, even though He sees our messy mess, mess, mess. His presence is what makes the Church a safe place; it is not the people in the Church who make or destroy the Church as a safe place. And His presence with us enables us to, like Him, wildly embrace all those around us in the Church, with their messes, while also speaking truth in love—all within the safety of the relationships Jesus is knitting together among us.

If that is our posture toward one another in the Body of Christ, what does Paul say our posture should be toward those outside the body of believers in Colossians 4:5?

"Outsiders" are those who live outside of Jesus' grace. This does not mean "outsiders" are loved less by God; rather, it means they do not have the same safety and security of relationship with Him that we do because of Jesus Christ. "Outsiders" may not know Jesus' grace and mercy at all, or they may be pushing Him away for vast and complicated reasons.

Who in your life is an outsider in this way? Write their name below, or draw a swipe of color that represents these people to you but leaves their name spoken only between you and God.

Take a few moments to pray for these dear people. Pray also that the Holy Spirit would help you make the best use of your time with them—whether that is giving you moments to talk about deep things of life and faith with them or moments to show them God's love and care in other ways. This looks different in different relationship, but regardless, you can be confident God will be faithful to give you opportunities to wildly love them.

Paul gives wisdom in Colossians 4:6 about one aspect of making the best use of the time. Write the verse in the space below.

Salt preserves and even nourishes. This makes salt a good analogy for God's Word, as well as for the relationship of God's people to the world where they live. In Colossians 4:6, Paul talks about speech being seasoned with salt, because salt makes things palatable.

MATTHEW 5:13
"You are the salt of the earth."

Have you ever had soup that the chef forgot to salt? Have you ever eaten meat with zero salt or seasoning? Tell about your saltless experience.

Food mess-ups because of a lack of salt are often good for a laugh. Communication mess-ups because of a lack of salt sometimes leave us laughing . . . but they can also leave us horrified (!). My favorite phrase for that kind of situation is this:

THERE'S GRACE FOR THAT.

COLOSSIANS 4:5
"Walk in wisdom toward those who are outside, redeeming the time." (NKJV)

The Holy Spirit does manage to make the best use of our time here on this earth. The Holy Spirit "redeems the time." Sometimes He helps us avoid communication heartache by nudging our conscience and causing us to pause an extra second to rethink what we were about to blurt out. Other times He redeems those instances when we mess up. Sometimes we see this visibly when we are able to confess, apologize, and be reconciled to the person we have hurt; we may even be able to laugh together with them about it eventually. But sometimes we have to wait patiently to see it redeemed, until the day when Jesus comes back and redeems everything, including our misspoken words. It can seem like a long time. But Jesus promises us He is always working, even when we don't see it.

In my communication, I have found that saltiness in the Spirit, speaking truth in wild amounts of love, looks particularly like the following four things:

- Boldness with tact
- Saying the right thing at the right time
- Saying the wrong thing at the wrong time, and the Spirit using it anyway
- Asking for forgiveness for the giant foot in my mouth or the mess I've made

Can you relate to one of these four areas more than the others?

I have made some progress in incorporating the above list into my daily communication. But I continue to need the Spirit every day. I continue to pray for a salty tongue because it is just so freakishly hard. In my prayers, in my communication in daily life, and in my sharing of the message and mercy of Jesus, I am thankful God seasons everything with His graciousness and wild amounts of His love.

Every time we communicate—in every prayer, every conversation, and every foot-in-mouth moment—God wraps His love around us and says:

THERE'S GRACE FOR THAT.

Connected by the Word

Use the Scripture memory verse for the week and the prayer prompt to bring your confession, thanksgiving, praise, and requests before our mighty and mysterious God.

Week 6 Memory Verse

Continue steadfastly in prayer, being watchful in it with thanksgiving. (Colossians 4:2)

Prayer Prompt

Holy Spirit, You live in my heart. Pour out gracious speech from my mouth; give me a salty tongue. Help me to let You reign in every part of my life . . .

Day 3

SENT TO ENCOURAGE
COLOSSIANS 4:7–9

During my first year in college, picking up my mail was one of the best parts of my day. Being away from home at college, while fun and adventurous, can be pretty lonely. There is so much that is new at that time—new people, new places, new bed, new schedule—that the longing for something familiar can quickly become an overwhelming feeling of sadness. I looked forward to mail time so much because it meant the possibility of something familiar from someone who knew me, loved me, and reminded me where I was from.

Each day at mail time, I'd stick my little key in my post office box and slowly open the little door. I'd reach inside and let out a little squeal of joy if I pulled out the gem of all college mail pieces: a colored envelope. The colored envelope meant someone had thought of me, whether back home or somewhere else that friends and family knew me. Someone had sat down and taken the time and energy to tell me that they were thinking of me and to ask how I was doing. The colored envelope was simple, but it was a huge burst of something every human being walking on this planet needs: encouragement.

Read Colossians 4:2–9. What does Paul say in these verses about the power of human words to encourage?

How have you been the recipient of words of encouragement within the Body of Christ?

AUTHOR'S NOTE
This is a very introspective scale. Be honest with yourself, knowing we are all imperfect. And remember: there's grace for that.

Salty tongues speak encouragement. On the scale of salty (gracious speech) to unsalty (speech lacking grace), where do you fall most of the time?

←————————————————————————————→

Salty   Unsalty

There is no shame here. We are all growing.

Part of the challenge in trying to have salty tongues that speak encouragement is that encouragement depends on more than what we say; it also depends on what is heard. What is encouraging for you may be different from what is encouraging for me. As we try to give authentic encouragement to others in the community of believers, we try to discern the weight and effect of our words on those we interact with, trying to be sensitive to where people are at emotionally, to the relationship we have with them, to past events in their lives that may have left them with scars only Jesus can see, and even to the events of the current day that may change what they need to hear or don't need to hear.

WE ARE ALL A COMPLICATED, MYSTERIOUS COMPILATION OF A PLETHORA OF NEEDS AND LIFE EXPERIENCES.

Whom do you regularly share words with, both inside and outside the Body of Christ?

In Colossians 4:7–9, we learn that Paul is sending his Letter to the Colossians by means of two trusted believers, Tychicus and Onesimus.

Tychicus: pronounced TIH-kih-kuhs

What reasons does Paul state in Colossians 4:7–9 for sending the letter by means of Tychicus and Onesimus?

Paul chose to have his letter hand-delivered to the Colossians by these two men whom he trusted, not only to ensure that the letter arrived safely, but also because Paul trusted Tychicus and Onesimus to accurately represent him to the Colossians. They not only would describe Paul's circumstances but also would *encourage* the Colossians' hearts by further explaining anything in the letter that might be confusing to the recipients. This reflects how human beings hear truth so much more effectively when it is spoken in the midst of a relationship where there is freedom to ask honest questions and have honest discussion.

It seems Paul trusts Tychicus not only because of Tychicus's proven character and faithfulness to Christ, but also because Paul believes the Holy Spirit will work through Tychicus as he speaks to the Colossians.

AUTHOR'S NOTE
It was not unusual for Paul to send a letter through one of his trusted fellow workers. See similar statements in the verses below:

1 Corinthians 16:10

Ephesians 6:21–22

Titus 3:12

What three characteristics does Paul apply to Tychicus in Colossians 4:7?

This is not the only time that Tychicus is mentioned in the New Testament. What do each of the following verses tell you about the relationship between Paul and Tychicus?

Acts 20:1–4

AUTHOR'S NOTE
There is a possibility that this Tychicus is not the one mentioned in Colossians 4:7. From my perspective though, the evidence stacks in favor of the Tychicus in these passages being the same as the one mentioned in Colossians.

Ephesians 6:21–22

2 Timothy 4:12

Titus 3:12

On day 5 last week, we mentioned that Paul's Letter to Philemon (written at about the same time as the Letter to the Colossians) helps us understand that Onesimus was a slave who had run away from his master Philemon.

What does Paul request of Philemon in Philemon 8–21?

Paul was sending Onesimus to Colossae for this reason as well as the reasons mentioned in Colossians 4:7–9. However, Paul's confidence in Onesimus as an important delegate to the Colossians, alongside Tychicus, shows Colossians 3:11 in action.

There's another important detail to notice in these verses. According to Colossians 4:9, what specific encouragement did Tychicus and Onesimus give to the Church at Colossae?

We so often try to encourage with our ideas or suggestions. One thing we can learn from this brief segment of Colossians is that words are often most encouraging when they simply report what God is doing in people's lives, including our own.

Think of an idea you have shared recently with a member of your local church, a friend, your spouse, or a co-worker. How could that idea be reframed to instead convey what God is doing in people's lives in relation to that idea?

We may not be sent expressly by someone like Paul to encourage another person or group of people. But we are sent by God to encourage the people around us, both inside and outside the Body of Christ, as He puts people into our lives and puts us in certain places at certain times. Sometimes our tongues are unsalty. But through Jesus we are forgiven. And through His constant care and feeding of us in the Church, we receive His encouragement in every possible way. The Spirit helps us grow so that we encourage one another in ways that reflect Jesus. In the midst of authentic relationships, we speak loving words of God's truth, paying attention to what would be most encouraging to our specific brothers and sisters in Christ at specific times.

Connected by the Word

Use the Scripture memory verse for the week and the prayer prompt to bring your confession, thanksgiving, praise, and requests before our mighty and mysterious God.

Week 6 Memory Verse

Continue steadfastly in prayer, being watchful in it with thanksgiving. (Colossians 4:2)

Prayer Prompt

Jesus, thank You for having a salty tongue with us and encouraging us every day. You know when our words are encouraging and when our words fail . . .

Day 4

ANNOYANCES, STRUGGLES, AND LIFE TOGETHER
COLOSSIANS 4:10–15

We have a recurring parking problem at our house:

- There is parking on only one side of our street.
- We have a street full of homes (including our home) overflowing with children and teenagers.
- We have a growing small-group Bible study at our house every Monday evening.

All of these details have created what we call the Monday parking shuffle.

It's kind of a nightmare, so, to try to make light of the situation, we joke as if the parking shuffle is a game. In this game, you attempt to find a parking spot near our house. You will probably drive around the block a couple of times trying to find a spot. Eventually, you might find a spot half a block away, or you might give up searching and finally decide to park in our driveway. But if you park in our driveway, you face the ten to one odds that the car you just blocked in will be needed to take a child to soccer practice or to make a run to the corner store for sweet cream for the cold brew. You have conquered the game when you get to sit down at our table with the other small-group members and with them study the Bible, laugh, have conversations, and do life together for a couple of hours in your week.

Once the parking challenge has been completed and we are all gathered together in my tiny living room/dining room with smiling faces, Bibles open, highlighters and pens out, discussing God's Word together, the annoyance of the parking shuffle is the furthest thing from our minds. And when we confront the parking shuffle again the following week, we bear with the annoyance because we know it yields something worthwhile.

Life together in the Church is often like our small-group study and the parking shuffle. There are plenty of annoying things in our life together, but they are worth the trouble. And sometimes these annoyances actually bring us together in ways we could not have anticipated or do not see at the time. Regardless, people are always worth the trouble.

As silly as my example sounds, the Monday parking shuffle is often the kind of annoyance that keeps people from gathering and doing life together in Christ. Other examples might be communication snafus between church members, too many people wanting to do the same job on a committee, not enough people wanting to do a job that needs to be done, or typos in the church newsletter.

What annoyances do you experience in life together in your local Body of Christ?

When annoyances start to threaten or harm others or our relationships with them, then they become serious struggles that we need to address with compassion, intentionality, and care. Paul knew about annoyances as well as serious struggles in life together in the Church.

Read Colossians 4:10–15 and list some of the annoyances and deeper struggles Paul addresses.

All kinds of things happen in the midst of our life together as the Church. Our sinfulness means we will not be able to avoid all annoyance or struggle in our life together. Yet we are still the Church, even in spite of and in the midst of our little and big struggles. Being Christ's Body is a reality Jesus established, not one that we established. Because we did not establish it, even our struggles do not get rid of it.

Yet Colossians 4:10–15 shows us that God does not ignore our specific problems and struggles in the Church. Did you notice how many specific people are mentioned in Colossians 4:10–15? These fellow workers are some of the massive cluster of marathon runners who surrounded the Colossians. Christ similarly puts people in our lives—people who are with us in worship at church, who discuss the Word with us in Bible study, who have coffee with us to hash out life's big questions—as visible reminders of the runners of faith all around us. And God promises to work in the midst of our specific annoyances and struggles with our specific fellow runners.

Reread Colossians 4:10–15, and list the names that are mentioned in these verses. These people are in the Colossians' cloud of witnesses:

Paul ends many of his letters by mentioning specific people like this. We shouldn't ignore these lists as if they are irrelevant for our place and time. They remind us that God cares about the specific connections He creates in

PHILIPPIANS 2:14–16
Paul gives important insight about how some of our typical responses to annoyances can have bigger effects than we realize:

"Do all things without grumbling or disputing, that you may be blameless and innocent, children of God without blemish in the midst of a crooked and twisted generation, among whom you shine as lights in the world, holding fast to the word of life, so that in the day of Christ I may be proud that I did not run in vain or labor in vain."

AUTHOR'S NOTE
Remember our discussion on day 1 this week of how perseverance in prayer is like being in a pack of marathon runners? It's a pretty good analogy for our whole Christian life, actually, not just prayer.

our lives and in His grand plan of salvation. Each name on the list has a story, and God cares about each one, just as He cares about each of our stories and how our stories are knit together. As I looked through the New Testament to learn as much about each of these individuals in Colossians 4:10–15 as I could, I was shocked by how much detail we actually do know about each of them. Let's look closer and be encouraged by some of their struggles, by the connections between our struggles and those of the Early Church, and by God's faithfulness in still holding them and us together in the Church. Grab your pen, your beverage of choice, and maybe a snack. A glimpse of life together in the New Testament is ahead!

ARISTARCHUS—COLOSSIANS 4:10

Aristarchus: pronounced ehr-ihs-TAHR-kuhs

According to Colossians 4:10, Aristarchus was a prisoner alongside Paul. Whether it means that he was arrested with Paul or that he volunteered to stand by Paul's side in prison to care for and encourage Paul, we don't know. We do know Paul and Aristarchus had a history of traveling and sharing the Gospel together as fellow workers.

Read the following passages. What connections and struggles did Paul and Aristarchus share in proclaiming the Gospel?

Acts 19:21–41

Acts 20:1–6

Acts 27:1–2

Being dragged away by a violent crowd because the Gospel is being preached is clearly more struggle than annoyance. Yet the fact that Aristarchus can send joyful greetings to the Colossians while being Paul's fellow prisoner in Colossians 4:10 reflects that suffering for the sake of the Gospel alongside our fellow Christians can bind us together in a way that is good even in the midst of suffering.

MARK—COLOSSIANS 4:10

If there was going to be a drama miniseries about the Early Church, I feel very confident there would be a plotline involving Mark, Barnabas's cousin.

I like to think of Mark as an imperfect missionary . . . but, then again, aren't we all? Mark's missionary stints appear to be brief. He comes and goes from Paul's missionary journeys, and sometimes it seems that trouble follows him.

What struggles and connections did Paul and Mark share together?

Acts 12:11–12, 25

Acts 13:5–13

Acts 15:36–39

We know Mark sided with Barnabas when Barnabas and Paul had a falling out. Did Mark do so because Barnabas had valid biblical points or because Barnabas was his cousin? There are questions that the Bible just doesn't answer for us, and this is one of them. It's beautiful to me, though, that Paul does not hold a grudge against Mark, despite his earlier frustration with Mark for abandoning the missionary journey and being on the opposite side in the disagreement with Barnabas. Rather, Paul honors Mark in Colossians 4:10. Note also the redemption in what Paul says of Mark in the following verse:

2 Timothy 4:11

This is an encouraging reminder to us that God does bring reconciliation and healing to complicated relationships. He can even bring such strong reconciliation that the people with whom we have a disagreement become all the more dear to us through that struggle.

Jesus/Justus—Colossians 4:11

At first glance, these names might be confusing. The man named Jesus whom Paul references in Colossians 4:11 is not Jesus Christ our Savior. Rather, this guy is a disciple named Jesus, who is also called Justus. *Jesus* was a relatively common name in the first century AD, a derivative of the Hebrew name *Joshua*. We don't know much about this particular man named Jesus/

> **AUTHOR'S NOTE**
> Mark has two names. It's common in the Bible, but it can be confusing for us when we study the Bible! You can find Mark mentioned by the names *Mark* and *John* . . . and sometimes *John Mark* . . . just to make it more fun and interesting.

Justus, except that Colossians 4:11 says he was circumcised, indicating that he was a Jewish convert to Christianity. Additionally, Paul says Jesus/Justus, alongside Aristarchus and Mark, has been a comfort to him. Comforting people is no small thing. Sometimes our words can be comforting, but often it is simply our presence that brings fellow members of the Body of Christ great comfort. It shows them that they are not alone. Our presence shows them God's love. Our presence is a physical reminder that God does not forsake us in our struggles. It is no small thing in the Body of Christ to have someone sit beside you.

EPAPHRAS—COLOSSIANS 4:12–13

We first met Epaphras in Colossians 1:7–8. What characteristics of Epaphras are described in Colossians 1:7–8 and Colossians 4:12–13?

Epaphras is a pastor to the Colossians. He has come to Paul and told Paul about some of the struggles among the Colossian believers. It seems Epaphras came to Paul, a mentor and leader in the Body of Christ, to seek advice about the situation in the Colossian Church. In Colossians 4:12–13, we learn that Epaphras has been praying with Paul about and for the Colossians. Epaphras cares about his people. Can you envision your pastor crying out to God on your behalf? I know a lot of pastors . . . *a lot*. And I don't know a single pastor who doesn't pray for the people God has asked him to love and care for. Pastors are flawed. Sometimes they don't know what to do about a situation, much like Epaphras. Sometimes pastors are a source of annoyance to us, since they are human and not perfect. Sometimes pastors mess up, speak harshly, or push their own agenda. But by God's grace, your pastor is struggling and wrestling *for you*, not against you.

What do you know about your pastor? What do you love about him? What struggles does he have? How can you pray for him today?

Epaphras's humility to come to Paul and ask for help resulted in so much good—for the Colossian Christians, for all Christians through time who have read Paul's letter, and even for us now. God is faithful to provide help for us in our struggles through other members of Christ's Body. What an incredible gift.

LUKE—COLOSSIANS 4:14

This "beloved physician" is the same Luke who wrote the Book of Acts and the Gospel of Luke. More than one commentator suggests that Luke may have tended to Paul physically during the missionary journeys recorded in Acts. Commentator Paul Deterding suggests Luke was present for the journeys recorded in Acts 16, Acts 20–21, and Acts 27–28 since the narrator uses "we" to describe Paul's travels.[15] Maybe Luke used his gifts as a physician to bandage Paul's wounds when he was beaten or to care for Paul when he was physically weakened by jail time or the wear of travel. Maybe Paul was encouraged by Luke's commitment to supporting the most important mission—the spread of the message of Christ's death and resurrection and the healing that only Jesus' forgiveness can bring. Maybe Luke proclaimed God's love, care, and forgiveness alongside Paul. Maybe Luke offered all of the above. Each of us are multifaceted bundles of gifts in the Body of Christ. Our gifts powerfully serve and encourage others in the Body, even when our gifts may not seem directly "spiritual."

What gifts has Christ given you to share with the rest of His Body?

DEMAS—COLOSSIANS 4:14

We have already seen that life in the church was hard in the first century, just as life in the church is hard in the twenty-first century. Some of the most painful times are when we don't see restoration or healing of what is broken. Sometimes we try very hard, but there are roadblocks to reconciliation that simply will not budge. God has not given us the ability nor the responsibility to force another person to allow broken pieces to be healed.

That is where Paul's relationship with Demas ends up. According to Colossians 4:14 and Philemon 23–24, Demas is among the fellow workers who have been very dear to Paul during his imprisonment. But by the time Paul wrote his second letter to his fellow worker Timothy, things had changed.

What evidence of brokenness do you find in 2 Timothy 4:9–10?

Sometimes people fall in love with this present world, trading eternity for what's working today. When one member of the Body falls in love with the world, the whole Body ends up heartbroken. The Body cries out to God and mourns for the Demases in our lives. We pray for them. We ache and struggle for them. And then we leave the matter in Jesus' lap, because we know He is struggling for them, interceding for them, even more than we ever could.

When we encounter brokenness that refuses to be healed, we don't shove it into some dark corner of our life together, as if it never existed or doesn't still exist. We look at it up close and personal and ask God what He is doing in our loss and in our sadness. Jesus knows our sorrow. He can handle our raw hurt, anger, frustration, and despair. Even when we don't see a situation or a relationship being healed, Jesus can heal our own hearts. Honesty with Him is where that begins. As you end your study time today, use the prayer prompt to pray for those you long to see in eternity. Jesus is interceding and praying for them just as you are. His promises are great. His promises are mighty.

The annoyances and deep struggles that Paul mentions in Colossians 4:10–15 about life together remind us:

WE ARE A MESS IN THIS BODY, BUT WE ARE HIS FORGIVEN, REDEEMED, LOVED, CALLED, CHOSEN, HONEST, REPENTING, DAILY-DYING AND DAILY-RISING MESS.

There will be annoyances in this life together. There will be deep struggles in this life together. When they occur, we lay them before our Savior. We ask Him to help us forgive one another through His forgiveness, to help us heal, and to help us love one another and invest in life together as His Body. Lord, hear our prayer.

Connected by the Word

Use the Scripture memory verse for the week and the prayer prompt to bring your confession, thanksgiving, praise, and requests before our mighty and mysterious God.

Week 6 Memory Verse

Continue steadfastly in prayer, being watchful in it with thanksgiving. (Colossians 4:2)

Prayer Prompt

Lord, You know every detail of our relationships and connections with those around us in the Body of Christ. You know the annoyances and struggles in our life together. Today I pray for . . .

Day 5

WHOSE CHURCH? JESUS' CHURCH
COLOSSIANS 4:16–18

Today let's connect one final time with Paul and with the Colossians. As we close our study, we remember that we are mysteriously connected to Paul, the Colossians, and the Christians of all times and places because we are one Body with them in Christ. As we talked about on day 1 this week, one way that we are connected to Christians of all times and places is through our prayers to our one mighty and mysterious Savior.

Can you notice in Colossians 4:16–18 another way that we are mysteriously connected to the Church at Colossae?

Paul and Timothy wrote the Book of Colossians to each of us just as much as to the Colossian Christians. They may not have understood the vastness of how God would use this letter in His Church, but they did intend for other Christians to read it. And by the power and inspiration of the Holy Spirit, God intends for the Letter to the Colossians to be His Word to Christians of all times and places.

Which Christians received the Book of Colossians not long after the Church in Colossae did, according to Colossians 4:16?

This is a cool glimpse into how the Gospel spreads and works among people. Paul traveled to Ephesus and preached the Gospel about Jesus there. Then someone took that message of hope in Jesus to someone else in Colossae. Someone else did the same for the nearby town of Laodicea. The Word of God went out from one person's life and touched another person. And that person connected yet another person to the Gospel. And pretty soon, there were brothers and sisters in Christ in Colossae and Laodicea worshiping Jesus and loving one another with the love they received from Him. And Paul had never even been to either of those places.

Whoa. God's Word and His work are very powerful.

MAP
See the map on page 14 to review the geography of this region and the proximity of these cities.

Nympha: pronounced NIHM-fa

In Colossians 4:15, we hear about a specific individual who was part of this, a person named Nympha. We don't know much about Nympha. But we do know that she offered the Lord and her family of faith a specific gift for the spread of the Gospel and life together in Christ.

What specific gift was that?

In what ways do we, as a congregation and as individuals, offer similar gifts of warmth, hospitality, and physical space today?

Nympha offered her home as a place where the Word could be read, heard, and discussed. Her home was a place where prayer could happen in safety and where believers could bear one another's struggles.

Where have you been blessed to go to hear the Word read in your life? Where have you been blessed to go to pray or to share struggles and burdens with others?

Sometimes these places are homes, sometimes they are empty halls with folding chairs, and sometimes they are church buildings with pews. But wherever God's Word is truthfully declared—God's Law convicting us, and the Gospel of Jesus forgiving all of our sins—there is Christ's Church. The Word is read and spoken, our ears hear it, our hearts believe it by God's gift of faith, and our burdens are laid down before Him. And there is rejoicing, singing, crying, laughing, and praying with our brothers and sisters as we receive the same gifts from God, being one Body in Christ.

This is a picture of the Church at Colossae. This is a picture of the Church at Laodicea. And this is a picture of your church and my church. Most important, this is a picture of *Jesus' Church*. He created, designed, planned, and founded it. He loves it, sends it out, feeds it, gives it His Spirit, and sustains it one day at a time until He comes again. Then He will bring His Church home as His Bride. Look at the beautiful relationship Paul describes between Jesus and His Church in Ephesians 5. Circle any phrase that describes Jesus' love for the Church:

Husbands, love your wives, as Christ loved the church and gave Himself up for her, that He

might sanctify her, having cleansed her by the washing of water with the word, so that He might present the church to Himself in splendor, without spot or wrinkle or any such thing, that she might be holy and without blemish.
(Ephesians 5:25–27)

Jesus loves His Church.

He would rather die than be without her. So, He came and died to make her His once again.

He is her Prince.

He is her Hero.

He is her Savior, her Friend, her Redeemer, her Guide.

In Colossians 4:17, Paul talks about one more specific individual in the Colossian Church: Archippus.

What is Paul's exhortation for Archippus in Colossians 4:17?

THE MYSTERY
Ephesians 5:32 reminds us that we won't always understand the mystery of this reality, but we certainly can stand on this description of Jesus' relationship with us:

"This mystery is profound, and I am saying that it refers to Christ and the church."

Archippus: pronounced ahr-KIHP-uhs

Archippus is also mentioned in Philemon 1–2. Circle how Archippus is described in those verses printed for you below:

Paul, a prisoner for Christ Jesus, and Timothy our brother, To Philemon our beloved fellow worker and Apphia our sister and Archippus our fellow soldier, and the church in your house.

The fact that Archippus is mentioned at the start of Paul's Letter to Philemon and in the second to last verse in Paul's Letter to the Colossians suggests that Archippus was a prominent figure among the Christians at Colossae. We don't know more than that. We are all like Archippus in that the Lord has given each of us something to do in this Body of Christ—a ministry that the Lord has given us to fulfill during our time on earth. We may not often think of it as a "ministry." But anything that serves others, that shows Jesus' love, and that points people to Him is a ministry that God has gifted us with in this short life.

What is your place and ministry that God has called you to right now?

Paul's words, then, are for us too:

See that you fulfill the ministry that you have received in the Lord. (Colossians 4:17)

We need what each person brings to the Church. It is life *together*, not life on our own. It wouldn't work the same with one person or one set of gifts missing.

Think of someone in the Body of Christ who has gifts that you treasure. How can you gently encourage that person to fulfill the ministry he or she has received from the Lord?

When we encourage others to fulfill the ministry God has given them, we are saying to them, "We need you in this church. You are valued here. You have a purpose. What would life be like without you? It wouldn't be the same without you. God sees what you bring to this Body, and so do I."

It is Jesus' Church. Throughout Colossians, we have learned what it looks like to live as Jesus' people in life together as His Church. The mystery that we are His people as His mighty gift—even though we are sinners, helpless, and messy—may overwhelm us at times. There is a command in it: we are called to bear this gift of being in Jesus' Church well. But what is even more mighty and mysterious is that His grace is stronger than our failures and our lack.

This is Jesus' Church. We are simply invited along. Everything in His Church abides in grace. So, Paul ends his letter to the Colossian Christians by speaking Jesus' powerful grace into their midst.

Fill in the missing words from Colossians 4:18 below. These are words for the Colossian Christians and for us:

I, Paul, write this greeting with my own hand. Remember my chains.

_____ _____ _____

_____.

I want all the grace. I *need* all the grace. You need all the grace.

ALL THE GRACE IS OURS IN JESUS CHRIST, THE MIGHTY ONE, THE MYSTERIOUS ONE.

I can't wait to see this mighty and mysterious God face-to-face. I can't wait for the mystery's full unveiling.

One day, when He comes back, we will see His mystery fully revealed and His might fully shown.

Until then, He does not desert us. Until then, He is among us through our relationships with one another—relationships strengthened by the diversity of thoughts, ideas, experiences, and backgrounds in the members of Christ's Body. Until then, He offers me arms to hold me up when I can't stand . . . through the members of His Body. He offers me hearts to hope when I can't hope . . . through the members of His Body. He offers me mouths to speak His Word over me when it's hard to trudge in the slush . . . through the members of His Body.

I am so thankful He is mighty. I am so thankful He is mysterious. I am so thankful He is Jesus. I am so thankful we are His Church.

As we end our study,

I, Heidi, write this with my own hand.

Remember that He binds us together—mercifully, purposefully, graciously, mightily, and mysteriously.

GRACE BE WITH YOU UNTIL THE DAY WHEN HE RETURNS FOR WHAT IS HIS.

> **1 Corinthians 12:14–20, 25**
> "For the body does not consist of one member but of many. If the foot should say, 'Because I am not a hand, I do not belong to the body,' that would not make it any less a part of the body. And if the ear should say, 'Because I am not an eye, I do not belong to the body,' that would not make it any less a part of the body. If the whole body were an eye, where would be the sense of hearing? If the whole body were an ear, where would be the sense of smell? But as it is, God arranged the members in the body, each one of them, as He chose. If all were a single member, where would the body be? As it is, there are many parts, yet one body . . . that there may be no division in the body, but that the members may have the same care for one another."

Connected by the Word

Use the Scripture memory verse for the week and the prayer prompt to bring your confession, thanksgiving, praise, and requests before our mighty and mysterious God.

Week 6 Memory Verse

Continue steadfastly in prayer, being watchful in it with thanksgiving. (Colossians 4:2)

Prayer Prompt

Jesus, You bring grace into my life and into Your Church . . .

Wrapped in Grace

30-DAY READING PLAN

Now that we have come to the end of our study, I'd like to offer you one more tool for connecting with Christ through His Word and His people. Each day, you can simply read the verse, or you can write it out to help you meditate on the grace we have in Christ. You might even text the verse to a friend to remind him or her as well as yourself that God wraps the grace of Jesus around each of us, around all of us, and all through the Body of Christ.

DAY 1
Colossians 1:2

DAY 8
1 Peter 4:10

DAY 2
Ephesians 2:8

DAY 9
2 Timothy 1:9

DAY 3
2 John 3

DAY 10
John 1:14

DAY 4
Romans 4:16

DAY 11
1 Corinthians 15:10

DAY 5
Philippians 1:7

DAY 12
2 Corinthians 1:15

DAY 6
Acts 4:33

DAY 13
Hebrews 4:16

DAY 7
Colossians 1:6

DAY 14
2 Thessalonians 1:12

DAY 15

Romans 5:2

DAY 16

Ephesians 3:8

DAY 17

James 4:6

DAY 18

John 1:16

DAY 19

Titus 2:11

DAY 20

1 Peter 5:10

DAY 21

Romans 5:15

DAY 22

1 Timothy 1:14

DAY 23

2 Corinthians 12:9

DAY 24

Hebrews 13:9

DAY 25

2 Timothy 2:1

DAY 26

Ephesians 4:29

DAY 27

Acts 11:23

DAY 28

1 Corinthians 16:23

DAY 29

Romans 6:14

DAY 30

Colossians 4:18

About the Author

Deaconess Heidi Goehmann is a licensed clinical social worker and mental health care provider, writer, speaker, wife, mom, and forgiven and loved child of God. She received her deaconess certification and her bachelor's degree in theology and psychology from Concordia University Chicago; her master's degree in social work is from the University of Toledo with an emphasis on children, families, and social justice.

Heidi can always be found at heidigoehmann .com, which provides resources and advocacy for mental health and genuine relationship.

Heidi loves her family, sticky notes, Jesus, adventure, Star Wars, Star Trek, and new ideas . . . not necessarily in that order.

A Note of Thanks

This book has been a season of wrestling for me. Thank you to Dave for being steady and full of grace when I am not, for valuing God's people so very much, and for dreaming wildly with me. I'm grateful to Sarah, Genevieve, Ali, and Jaime, who walk through life with me every day and discern the Word alongside me. Thank you for letting me ask questions, throw out ideas, and sort through what the Body of Christ is, what it is not, and what I want it to be, in honesty and authenticity. Thank you for not being afraid of the slush.

Thank you to Macee, Jonah, Jyeva, and Zeke for sitting by my desk for a chat, playing beside me with Legos while I typed, and encouraging me to write braver every day.

Thank you to Alexa, Laura, Holli, Lindsey, Elizabeth, Loren, Alex, and the entire CPH team for answering my million emails and always treating me like one of the family. Thank you to Gabe, Kathy, and the film crew for their insight, expertise, and kind support.

Thank you to each of the congregations who have raised up Dave and I and our family. Thank you to the friends who have sat around our table, willing to do life together. Thank you to each of our people who have wept with us, laughed with us, celebrated with us, and played dominos with us into the wee hours of the morning. This is His Body, and I am eternally grateful to be a part of it.

Endnotes

1   John R. W. Stott, " 'In Christ': The Meaning and Implications of the Gospel of Jesus Christ," *Knowing & Doing* (Summer 2007): 18–23, http://www.cslewisinstitute.org/In_Christ_page1.

2   Paul E. Deterding, *Colossians*, Concordia Commentary (St. Louis, MO: Concordia Publishing House, 2003), 23.

3   Bible Hub, s.v. "40. hagios," http://biblehub.com/greek/40.htm.

4   Dr. Christopher Mitchell, personal communication with author, July 23, 2018.

5   See, for example, Warren W. Wiersbe, *The Wiersbe Bible Commentary: The Complete Old Testament in One Volume* (Colorado Springs, CO: David C. Cook, 2007), 658.

6   Jurgen Appelo, "Ditch the Praise Sandwich, Make Feedback Wraps," Forbes.com, August 17, 2015, https://www.forbes.com/sites/jurgenappelo/2015/08/17/ditch-the-praise-sandwich-make-feedback-wraps/#24e816db-fa4a.

7   Deterding, *Colossians*, 35.

8   Max Anders, *Galatians, Ephesians, Philippians, and Colossians*, Holman New Testament Commentary (Nashville, TN: Broadman and Holman Publishers, 1999), 283, provides this explanation in light of how the word for "image" was used and understood in the time of the New Testament.

9   JoHannah Reardon, "The Nicene and Apostles' Creeds," Christianity Today, July 30, 2008, https://www.christianitytoday.com/biblestudies/articles/churchhomeleadership/nicene-apostles-creeds.html.

10 Christian Cyclopedia, s.v. "Ecumenical Creeds," http://cyclopedia.lcms.org/display.asp?t1=e&word=ECUMENICALCREEDS.

11 Deterding, *Colossians*, 66.

12 Johann Hari, "Everything You Think You Know about Addiction Is Wrong," TED Talk, June 2015, https://www.ted.com/talks/johann_hari_everything_you_think_you_know_about_addiction_is_wrong.

13 Austin Channing Brown, *I'm Still Here: Black Dignity in a World Made for Whiteness* (New York, NY: Convergent Books, 2018), 118.

14 Bob Goff, *Love Does* (Nashville, TN: Thomas Nelson, 2012), 80–81, 83.

15 Deterding, *Colossians*, 188.

16 Bible Hub, s.v. "80. adelphos," http://biblehub.com/greek/80.htm.

17 Bible Hub, s.v. "4336. proseuchomai," http://biblehub.com/greek/4336.htm.

18 Bible Hub, s.v. "154. aiteó," https://biblehub.com/greek/154.htm.

19 Bible Hub, s.v. "4409. próteuó," http://biblehub.com/greek/4409.htm.

20 Bible Hub, s.v. "526. apallotrioó," http://biblehub.com/greek/526.htm.

21 Bible Hub, s.v. "3884. paralogizomai," http://biblehub.com/greek/3884.htm.

22 Bible Hub, s.v. "4138. pléróma," http://biblehub.com/greek/4138.htm.

23 Bible Hub, s.v. "4137. pléroó," http://biblehub.com/greek/4137.htm.

24 Bible Hub, s.v. "3856. paradeigmatizó," https://biblehub.com/greek/3856.htm.

25 Bible Hub, s.v. "2212. zétéo," https://biblehub.com/greek/2212.htm.